MW01602301

COMMON CORE

To Janny,

In appreciation
of your support
+ all you do
in literacy!

COMMON CORE

Using Global Children's Literature and Digital Technologies

Paula Saine

ROWMAN & LITTLEFIELD
Lanham • Boulder • New York • London

Published by Rowman & Littlefield
A wholly owned subsidiary of
The Rowman & Littlefield Publishing Group, Inc.
4501 Forbes Boulevard, Suite 200, Lanham, Maryland 20706
www.rowman.com

Unit A, Whitacre Mews, 26-34 Stannary Street, London SE11 4AB

Copyright © 2016 Paula Saine

All rights reserved. No part of this book may be reproduced in any form
or by any electronic or mechanical means, including information storage
and retrieval systems, without written permission from the publisher,
except by a reviewer who may quote passages in a review.

British Library Cataloguing in Publication Information Available

Library of Congress Cataloging-in-Publication Data Available

ISBN 978-1-4758-1353-1 (cloth : alk. paper)
ISBN 978-1-4758-1354-8 (pbk. : alk. paper)
ISBN 978-1-4758-1355-5 (electronic)

∞™ The paper used in this publication meets the minimum requirements
of American National Standard for Information Sciences—Permanence of
Paper for Printed Library Materials, ANSI/NISO Z39.48-1992.

Printed in the United States of America

This book is dedicated to my sisters, Sheila, Gale, and Nette, and to our mother, Viney, for always being there for me.

This book is dedicated to the memories of my dad, Leroy, and my brother, Dedrick.

CONTENTS

ACKNOWLEDGMENTS

In researching and writing this book, I have benefited from the generous assistance of several colleagues and graduate students in the Department of Teacher Education, whose comments, feedback, and suggestions throughout the various stages of the process proved invaluable. I wish to thank Alundra Childs, Genesis Ross, Ryan McCarthy, Gavin Pond, Theresa Williams, Jenna Halsey, and Mary Beth Alexander for their assistance on an earlier draft of this book. To Crystal Alridge and Brittany Beaver who assisted me in gathering student work samples, I will always be grateful. This project also benefited from the input of Leslie Robson, Jana Orwig, and Tami Richardson. To my colleague Iris Johnson, for her unflinching support and commitment to my work over the years, I express my profound gratitude. To my husband, Abdoulaye Saine, and our children, I thank you for your support, love, and understanding. I also wish to express profound appreciation to my editors, Sarah Jubar, Christine Fahey, Carlie Wall, and Laura Reiter. Because of their suggestions through the different stages of writing, this book is a better product. I dedicate this book to all current and future teachers as they work to engender literacy, culture, and digital technologies in the classroom environment. And to the children they teach, this book was written with you in mind, that you may grow to appreciate this diverse and global world we live in!

1

INTRODUCTION

OVERVIEW

Common Core: Using Global Children's Literature and Digital Technologies focuses on nine regions of the world and is fundamentally connected to three tenets: literacy, culture, and the use of digital technology for enhancing deeper understanding in elementary classroom curriculum. Through the use of this book, teachers can explore and begin to diversify their selection of global and multicultural literature from various regions of the world and underrepresented ethnic communities of the United States.

Classrooms of the twenty-first century continue to become more culturally diverse and require that both teachers and students think strategically to be more global minded. Teachers, therefore, have a huge responsibility not only to keep abreast of technological changes to impact the literacy curriculum but also to access these technologies to engender global mindedness in students, equipping them with tools for intrinsically inspired cross-cultural awareness.

This book focuses on how teachers can draw upon their students' background knowledge (Anderson and Pearson 1984) and cultural experiences (Lee 2005) to construct meaning (Piaget 1963; Vygotsky 1978) and respond to literature (Rosenblatt 1978) while incorporating digital technologies literacy learning (Leu, Kinzer, Coiro, and Cammack 2004; Abadiano and Turner 2007; Gooch and Saine 2011). Through this process, students will be empowered by their ideas and, with appropriate support, they will develop critical insights into what they know about our global society through writing genres such as letter, persuasion, description, exposition, and poetry.

The written responses will be extended using multiple digital technologies. It has been found that student learning is positively influenced when the student uses electronic tools as he/she actively engages in the learning process (Boxie 2004; Boxie and Maring 2001; Saine and Kara-Soteriou 2010). Moreover, Karchmer, Leu, Mallette, and Kara-Soteriou (2005) posit how teachers see the benefits of using technology to help students deepen their understanding of literature through reading, writing, listening, and speaking.

LITERACY

Literacy instruction is much more than giving students quality literature; it is doing the authentic things (reading, writing, sharing, talking, and thinking) with the literature that all writers and readers would naturally do, and giving students support with these activities as they need it. For example, it is natural to share and talk about a good book after reading it; it is not natural to answer ten questions about a book. As teachers, our role is one of planning and supporting authentic literacy experiences for our students.

A major goal of K–3 teachers is to ensure that the students are able to read with meaning and are able to comprehend what they read. Therefore, the literacy activities in the classroom should include aspects of reading, writing, language, speaking, and listening (Tyner 1998). Additionally, literacy instruction should contain a selection of literature from authors who provide the students with the opportunity to identify with characters, events, and emotions that are similar to their own personal experiences.

For example, in *Sofie and the City* (2006) by Karima Grant, the young girl, Sofie, recently moved to New York from the country of Senegal, West Africa, and was unhappy with the move until she found a new friend. Many students may have experienced this same experience of moving or may know someone who shares this cultural experience.

As students attempt to understand and to make meaning of the texts and biographies, it is important for teachers to embed reading comprehension strategies in their instruction. This involves students monitoring their understanding before, during, and after reading activities to build prior knowledge and schema to enhance comprehension.

Biography summary is also a great tool to use to assist students in retrieving important information from texts. Students can use this strategy to break down biographies into smaller chunks so they can have a better understanding of an individual's life. For example, students can examine biographies to determine how Nelson Mandela's character developed throughout his life. Other instruction activities include but are not limited to building background knowledge; demonstrating an understanding of vocabulary; clarifying the meaning of unknown words; writing poetry, arguments, and informative and narrative pieces; and conducting research.

CULTURAL COMPETENCE/GLOBAL MINDEDNESS

As teachers facilitate their own development as culturally responsive literacy teachers, they begin to carefully select books that can bring all cultures in their classroom together. Pang (2001) defined culturally relevant teaching as "an approach to instruction that responds to the sociocultural context and seeks to integrate cultural content of the learner in shaping an effective learning environment" (p. 192). In addition, they will come to realize that their understanding of reading and how literature, which reflects "mirrors" of our own lives and "windows" into the lives of others, can enrich all of our lives.

Sims-Bishop (1990) argues that books are windows offering views of our world that may be real or imagined, familiar or strange, and when lighting conditions are just right, a window can also be a mirror reflecting our own lives and experiences as part of the larger human experience (p. ix). All students, Violet Harris (1997) writes, feel welcome in school to the extent that they find themselves and their experiences represented in the books and materials read there.

One way to prepare diverse students to be global minded is by carefully varying the range and selection of global and multicultural children's literature. In fact, McKenna (2007) not only argues succinctly that all voices should be heard, but also states that "our students cannot know the world in which they live without the perspectives of the people who populate it" (p. 183).

When teachers incorporate global literature into the literacy curriculum throughout the school year, this not only aids students in gaining a better sense of the world but also assists in transcending cultural stereotypes in the world in which they live. Global literatures, as defined by Hadaway and McKenna (2007), "is a comprehensive and inclusive one, representing literature that honors and celebrates diversity, both within and outside the United States. . . . [It] includes both multicultural and international literature" (p. 5).

A popular and reliable website for promoting literature is Worlds of Words (http://wowlit.org/). This site is at the University of Arizona in the College of Education, where teachers will find an estimated thirty thousand volumes of children's and adolescent literature focusing on world cultures and indigenous peoples. Articles are also available for accessing global literature for classroom use.

For example, Asia Society (Children's Literature Builds Global Competence; http://asiasociety.org/education/resources-schools/professional-learning/childrens-literature-builds-global-competence) currently contains eight interactive online books for children to utilize and has a list of books from different cultures. After reading these global books, students can respond to literature by recounting the story, comparing and contrasting stories, or searching for common themes across books (Saine and Kara-Soteriou 2010).

DIGITAL TECHNOLOGY

Like the importance of teacher preparedness for culturally and linguistically diverse populations, the infusion of technology into the curriculum is increasingly important. Leu and Kinzer (2000) argue that the competition in global economics is driving the infusions and changes in digital technologies in the classroom. Due to these changes, literacy in reading, writing, and communication are also changing. Therefore, teachers of literacy must explore innovative and engaging ways of using multiple digital technologies such as audio, enhanced and video podcasting, digital storytelling, and PowerPoint to promote cultural competence and literacy instruction in their classroom.

A podcast is simply a digital audio or video file (usually MP3 or MP4) made available on the Internet with a news feed or a really simple syndication (RSS). The ability to capture one's voice is an amazing way to enhance student writing skills as students prepare to report reading and writing for a larger audience through podcasts. In doing so, students can use Audacity, which is a free software and is cross-platform.

Increasingly, the Internet has given teachers access to shared digital spaces and online resources for enhancing literacy instruction. For instance, Education World (http://www.educationworld.com/) is a shared space available to teachers each day to locate high-quality content material for use in the classroom. In addition, CNN Student News and Radio broadcasts (www.broadcast-live.com) are free online resources that enable both students and teachers to access global news websites and radio stations around the world.

These news outlets can also create deeper discussions as multiple perspectives are shared. However, reading the headlines from any source requires critical thinking to make important distinctions between what is deemed worthy and what appears to be trivial or sometimes propaganda.

Blogging and Twitter are also useful tools for older students to use when learning from and about others. One credible site I recommend for using social media (that is, blogging, tweeting, Pinterest, Facebook, LinkedIn, email) is Development in Action (www.developmentinaction.org). Through blogging, students from different cultures of the world can actively engage in discussing current events and controversial global issues that center on international development. In these instances, teachers and students can be connected to resources they need to promote ongoing dialogue with citizens from other cultures who serve as experts about their own countries.

INTENT OF THIS BOOK

One of the major reasons for writing this book is to assist teachers to overcome obstacles they face when using global and multicultural literature. Another reason is to overcome the lack of knowledge of a country and/or its culture(s). Therefore, to help transcend these cultural barriers, I provide a section on country background that contains historical, economic, and political information, as well as web resources and apps for both students and teachers.

The countries are organized alphabetically, with each chapter featuring literacy (reading, writing, speaking, and/or listening) activities and digital technologies. I chose to organize the book by geographic region rather than by literacy competencies because it would be beneficial for teachers when using theme-based lessons.

If teachers are provided with all the tools for implementing global and multicultural children's literature and those tools are aligned with Common Core Standards, they are more likely to implement this type of literature into instruction. At the end of each chapter, teachers are provided related apps and web resources with QR codes that navigate to cultural informational websites.

Importantly, this book is intended for college professors, current and future K–3 classroom teachers, literacy coaches, and parents (homeschool). It can be used as a primary or secondary text in a college methods course as well. The book may also be used during professional development meetings as a tool for enhancing culturally responsive teaching.

I invite readers to explore innovative and engaging ways of using digital technologies such as Google Earth, podcasting, digital storytelling, iBooks Author, Glogster, StoryBird, Diigo, online newspapers, apps, and so on. In so doing, this book provides multiple technology resources and tips for teachers of literacy at the end of each chapter.

The selection of global and multicultural children's books contains genres such as fiction, nonfiction, poetry, and so on. Embedded in each chapter are literacy and digital activities to enable both students and teachers to become more aware of the world around them. However, teachers may also choose to organize according to the themes of books or specific literacy competencies. I encourage readers to explore these titles as they begin to diversify the selections in their own classrooms.

This chapter presents an overview of research behind implementation of literacy, culture, and use of digital technology for enhancing deeper understanding of various cultures in the elementary classroom curriculum.

The four African works featured in chapter 2 are *Fatuma's New Cloth* (2002) by Leslie Bulion, *My Father's Shop* (2006) by Satomi Ichikawa, *Sofie and the City* (2006) by Karima Grant, and *Mandela: From the Life of a South Africa Statesman* (1996) by Floyd Cooper. They explore stories of East Africa, Morocco, Senegal, and South Africa.

Students will travel to East Africa to discover with Fatuma that you cannot always see the good things that are on the inside, learn foreign words with Mustafa as he visits his friends in the market in Morocco, find out how Sofie becomes happy again after her move from Senegal to New York, and follow Mandela's journey in becoming a leader in South Africa. Using Rosenblatt's principles of reader response theory, students can read and respond to global and multicultural children's literature of this region of the world.

The activities are connected to Common Core English Language Arts Standards and engage students in building background knowledge; descriptive word banks; making connections; fictional, descriptive, persuasive, and poetry writings; and research.

Similarly, chapter 3 feature works from five North Asian countries. The five north Asian works, *My Chinatown: One Year in Poems* (2002) by Kim Mak, *A Song for Ba* (2004) by Paul Yee, *Kamishibai Man* (2005) by Allen Say, *Suki's Kimono* (2003) by Chieru Uegaki, and *Halmoni's Day* (2000) by Edna Bercaw, explore stories of China, Japan, and South Korea.

Students will listen to poems to learn about two Chinese cultures (Hong Kong and Chinatown, USA), Wei's desire to sing in the Chinese opera like his father and grandfather, Jiichan's passion of storytelling in a changing world, Suki's excitement to share her cultural experience on the first day of school, and a Korean American girl named Jennifer's apathy in sharing her culture on Grandparents' Day. The activities engage students in building background and word knowledge; retelling; synonyms; compound words; sentence, letter, story (point of view), and report writings; and research.

In chapter 4, children's books from Bangladesh, India, Indonesia, and Afghanistan are highlighted. The four works of South Asia—*Basket of Bangles: How a Business Begins* (2002) by Ginger Howard, *Monsoon* (2003) by Uma Krishnawami, *Rice Is Life* (2000) by Rita Gelman, and *Four Feet, Two Sandals*

(2007) by Karen Williams—explore the cultures of Bangladesh, India, Indonesia, and Afghanistan.

Students will travel to Bangladesh and discover the steps taken by Sufiya and her friends for starting a new business, in India they will learn about the monsoon, in Bali the importance of rice and how it grows as the animals take part in the life cycle, and in Afghanistan how two Afghani girls living in a refugee camp share their stories of grief and hope over the simple act of sharing one pair of sandals. The activities engage students in building background and vocabulary knowledge; checking predictions; story sequencing; summarizing; compounds words; persuasive letter; and expository writings; and research.

The four Caribbean works featured in chapter 5, *Circles of Hope* (2005) by Karen Williams, *Under the Breadfruit Tree: Island Poems* (1998) by Monica Gunning, *Rata-Pata-Scata-Fata: A Caribbean Story* (2005) by Phyllis Gershator, and *Fish for the Grand Lady* (2006) by Colin Bootman, which explore the cultures of the Caribbean islands of Haiti, Jamaica, St. Thomas, and Trinidad and Tobago.

Students will travel to Haiti with Facile to discover why it is challenging for him to plant a tree. Next, they can travel to Jamaica and see how Monica Gunning uses descriptive poetry to tell the story of a Jamaican family and their friends. In St. Thomas, they will become familiar with a young boy named Junjun, who believes that uttering a few special words will help him get his chores done. Finally, they can meet Derrick and Colly, of Trinidad and Tobago, who want to do something special for their grandmother, the "Grand Lady." The activities engage students in building background knowledge; making predictions; sequencing; book review, fictional, descriptive, and poetry writings; and research.

The European works featured in chapter 6 are *My Name Was Hussein* (2004) by Hristo Kyuchukov, *Boxes for Katje* (2003) by Candace Fleming, *In English, Of Course* (2002) by Josephine Nobisso, and *The Hungry Coat: A Tale from Turkey* (2004) by Demi. These authors explore stories of Bulgaria, Holland, Italy, and Turkey, respectively. It should be noted that while Turkey is typically classified as a country in Asia, in this book I classify it under Europe because it lies between Europe and Asia.

Three of the five stories are based on true experiences and students will note various cultural challenges. For example, in *My Name Was Hussein*, Hussein and his Muslim family experience the injustice of religious prejudice. In *Boxes for Katje*, Fleming sheds light on the needs of a Dutch family after the war and then teaches the importance of sharing and caring for others. Finally, in the story *In English, Of Course*, Nobisso touches the hearts of the readers who are learning how to express themselves using a language that is not their own. In the work from Turkey, Demi teaches the readers about how important it is to see a person from the inside and not to judge from the surface.

The activities engage students in making predictions; identifying character traits; practicing phrase and expressive reading; story mapping; antonyms; story (point of view); identifying parts of the story; letter, poetry, and message writing; digital storytelling; and research.

The Central American works featured in chapter 7, *Jahmon's Adventure Home* (2006) by Bill Hash and *Alfredito Flies Home* (2007) by Jorge Arugueta, explore the cultures of Belize, Cost Rica, and El Salvador. Students will travel to Belize to join Jahmon in this imaginative tale about a boy lost from home. Another great book they can read is *The Remembering Stone* by Barbara T. Russell (2004). With the creative use of Spanish words and phrases throughout the English text of the book, the author tells the story of a young girl named Ana and her mother, whose dream is to return to her home country of Costa Rica. Finally, students can travel with Alfredito and his family as they return to El Salvador, their original home, to visit family. The activities engage students in building background and word knowledge, comparing and contrasting cultures, realistic and fantasy events, letter and narrative writings, and research.

The North American works featured in chapter 8 are *A Sweet Smell of Roses* (2005) by Angela Johnson, *The Other Side* (2001) by Jacqueline Woodson, *Jingle Dancer* (2000) by Cynthia Smith, *The Good Luck Cat* (2000) by Joy Harjo, *Family* (2005) by Isabell Monk, *Am I a Color Too?* (2005) by Heidi Cole and Nancy Vogl, *The Pot That Juan Built* (2002) by Nancy Andrews-Goebel, and *I Love Saturdays y Domingos* (2002) by Alma Ada Flor. Each book showcases stories of underrepresented ethnic and racial communities including African Americans, Native American/Muscogee, Asian Americans, an interracial category, and Mexican Americans. The activities engage students in building background and word knowledge; understanding personification; identifying character traits and poetic forms; writing sentences, ads, book reviews, a letter, and an invitation; and research.

The South American works featured in chapter 9—*Brazil* (2008) by Elizabeth Weitzman, *My Name Is Gabito* (2007) by Monica Brown, *Tomasino: A Child of Peru* (2005) by Herve Giraud, and *Venezuela ABCs* (2007) by Sharon Cooper—explore stories of Brazil, Columbia, Peru, and Venezuela.

In the first book, students will learn about Brazil as well as enjoy this short chapter book that covers a wide variety of topics about its culture and life. When reading *My Name Is Gabito*, they will see how author Monica Brown brings the powerful imagination and compassion of Gabito to life though this beautifully illustrated book that is told in English and Spanish. In *Tomasino: A Child of*

Peru, the author gives a snapshot into the life of Tomasino, a young Quechuan Indian boy who lives in Peru. Finally, Sharon Cooper's book explores the unique beauty and traditions of Venezuela through use of the alphabet. The activities engage students in alphabetizing and learning Brazilian vocabulary, questioning strategy, visualizing, sequencing important events, comparing and contrasting, completing sentences, informative and poetry writings, and research.

Together, the books are an important attempt to overcome cultural barriers and assist both teachers and students in enhancing cultural literacy competencies.

❷

AFRICA

EAST AFRICA
Fatuma's New Cloth **by Leslie Bulion (2002)**
Grade Levels: K–3
Themes: Family, Market, Clothes

Summary:

Fatuma goes to the market with Mama and meets many people who sell tea and spices, milk, and pans, who all claim their goods will help make a better chai. But Fatuma wonders how Mama can make hers sweeter. When they get to the kanga shop Fatuma looks for the perfect kanga for herself, and when she finds the right color, she finds the answer to the perfect chai written on the cloth: "*Don't be fooled by the color. The good flavor of chai comes from the sugar.*" Then Fatuma realizes that you cannot always see the good things because they are on the inside, and it is true not just for sugar but for people as well.

Country Information:

Located on the eastern coast of Africa, the Republic of Kenya has a warm tropical climate and some areas of desert-like conditions. The people of Kenya, called Kenyans, are ethnically diverse (a majority being Kikuyu, Luyia, or Luo), and many languages are widely spoken. English is the official language, but Swahili is commonly heard and, to a lesser extent, traditional languages are also spoken. Kenyans are predominately Christian (80 percent), but Islam and traditional religions are also practiced.

Kenya is a republic with three branches of government: executive, legislative, and judicial. Because of the unfortunate current political upheaval in the country, temporary changes to government positions have been made to keep the peace. Because education is a concern for the country, the first eight years of school are paid for by the government, which makes for a high attendance rate in the primary grades (92 percent).

However, adult literacy is still problematic (only about 85.1 percent of Kenyans are literate). The major source of income in Kenya is through service works, even though Kenya is an agriculturally based country. The major crops are tea, coffee, and sugar cane. Livestock is also an important part of Kenya's economy.

LITERACY ACTIVITIES

Markets and Supermarkets

RL.K.1, RL.1.1, RL.2.1, RL.3.1

Ask the students what they know about Kenya, East Africa. List responses on chart paper. Use Google Earth or a map, globe, or app to locate Kenya, East Africa. Explain how some people in Kenya make a living. Discuss the different types of things that might be sold at the market.

Ask students if there is a market where they live or if they have visited an African market before. Explain to students that oftentimes when people shop in an African market, the prices are negotiable (they are not fixed but are able to be established or changed through discussion and compromise). Ask if they have a supermarket where they shop. Have students share some of the things their parents or guardians have purchased at the supermarket. Ask students if the prices at the supermarket are negotiable.

Have the students use a Venn diagram (appendix A) in small groups to compare and contrast the benefits of shopping at the market versus shopping at the supermarket. Have students display their Venn diagram in the classroom.

Supermarket Dictation

SL.K.1

Because most students take trips to the grocery store with their family, talk about what they do while they are there, what they see, and/or what they buy at the store. Discuss with the students items they would sell if they were the owner of a supermarket. Then use the following sentence starter and have them dictate their responses to the teacher before recording it using the Dictation app on an iPad. They will say, "If I owned a supermarket, I would sell _____."

Character Traits

RL1.3, RL2.3, RL3.3

Fatuma's mother talked about the fact that things that are found on the inside are not always seen on the outside. Ask students how they see or think about themselves. Have students think about who they are by writing words that describe their character traits. Discuss inside (invisible) and outside (visible) characteristics. Have them revisit the list of descriptive words and sort them according to "visible" or "invisible" characteristics (see figure 2.1).

Finally, have them create a class podcast or eBook by having students tell about themselves. For example, a student might write and say, "One of my invisible characteristics is that I am a thinker." "One of my visible characteristics is that I have black hair."

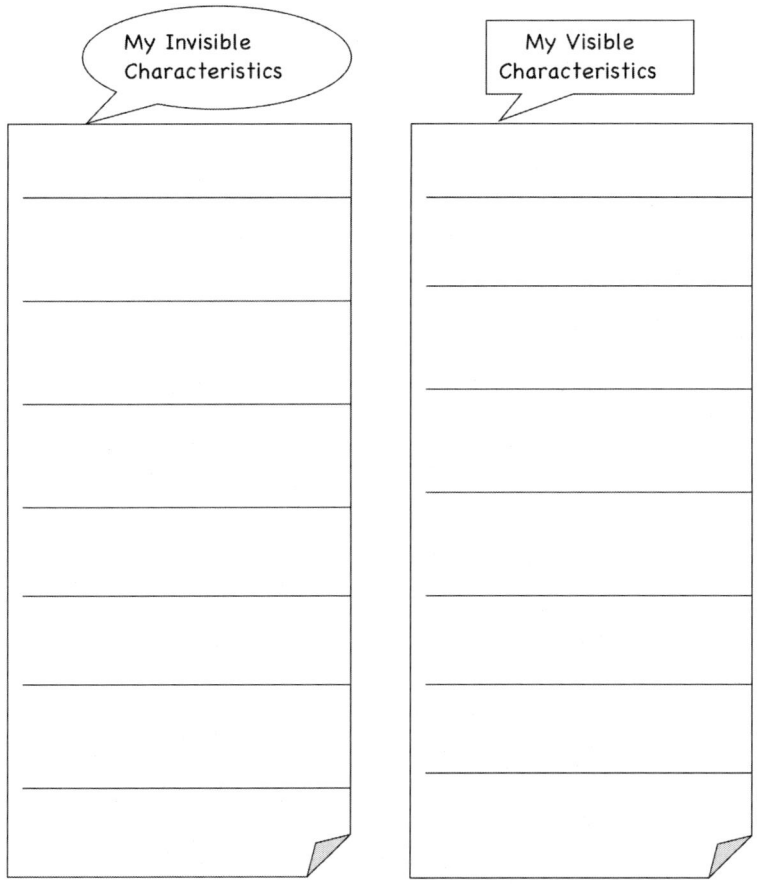

Figure 2.1.   Sorting Descriptive Words

Using Metaphors

L.2.5, L.3.5

Fatuma wanted a kanga that was the "color of the deep sea and the early morning sky." A kanga is a brightly colored and decorated piece of cotton cloth that women wrap over their dresses as a garment to protect them from dust and cooking stains. Fatuma would wear a play dress made from a piece of folded kanga.

Have the students think about the writing Fatuma found on the kanga: *"Don't be fooled by the color. The good flavor of chai comes from the sugar."* (It also means that "you can't judge a book by its cover" or "you can't tell whether people are good by looking at them.") Ask students what they thought about when they heard the words. Have them explain what it means to them. Then students work in small groups or pairs to come up with two more metaphors they could write on the kanga that they would like to design.

Persuasive Writing

W.2.1, W.3.1

Tell the students they will work individually or in small groups as they write and record a persuasive paragraph, as shown in figure 2.2, in which they will pretend they are the owner of a shop in the market. The purpose of the paragraph is to persuade Fatuma to buy cloth at their shop.

Remind students that when they try to persuade someone, it means that they try to get the other person to see things their way. They can begin this process using the app "Writing an Opinion." When their paragraphs are completed, students can begin creating an enhanced podcast using voice, music, and Google images.

The Fabulous Cloth Market

Welcome to the Fabulous Cloth Market (FCM). My shop is very special because I have hundreds of different selections of cloth you can choose from. Since this weekend is Father's Day, all cloth is 50% off and that means all cloth is $1.00. We even have new cloth in all colors. Some with stripes, dots, zigzag, glitter and specifically some with diamonds that spell out "Dad." And best of all, if you don't like the selection of cloth in my shop, then you can come to our custom booth and design your own.

Come to the FCM
TODAY!!!

Figure 2.2. Persuasive Writing

Spotlight Kenya

SL.2.5, SL.3.5

Have students produce an episode on Kenya, East Africa, for the class weekly, bi-weekly, or monthly radio show. Student groups will create MP3 (Audacity) or MP4 (video) digital files to (1) report a glimpse of Kenya's geography, history, and culture and (2) share the summary of Kenyan book(s) read.

MOROCCO
My Father's Shop by Satomi Ichikawa (2006)
Grades K–3
Themes: Shops, Market, Tourists, Languages

Summary:

Mustafa's father sells beautiful rugs in his shop in Morocco, where tourists often visit. One day, when Mustafa finds a rug with a hole, his father gives it to him in exchange for a promise that he will learn foreign words from his father. Mustafa, however, runs out of the shop after one lesson and visits his friends in the market when a rooster starts following him.

When one of his friends asks him to make the rooster sing, he says, "Kho Kho Hou Houuu," the way roosters crow in Morocco. Then various tourists come and join in and show how roosters sing in their country. Excited that he learned lots of foreign words, he runs back to his father's shop and, without realizing, he brings in all the tourists with him. Ichikawa's colorful artwork blends in with Mustafa's cheerful character.

Country Information:

The Kingdom of Morocco is a mountainous region with many plateaus and lush coastal borders. Morocco is a warm country with higher temperatures in the southern portion. Most Moroccans are descendants of both Arab and Berber ethnic groups. The official language is Arabic, but Berber dialects can be heard.

As Morocco is a former protectorate of France, French is spoken there, but it is mostly heard in matters related to business, government, and commerce. The vast majority of the population of Morocco is Muslim, but small numbers of Jews and Christians live in the country.

The Moroccan government is a constitutional monarchy with a bicameral (meaning "two houses," comparable to the U.S. Senate and the House of Representatives) legislature. Education for children is mandatory for the first nine years, but the overall literacy rate is 68.5 percent. Moroccan industry focuses on public service jobs, phosphate mining, manufactured goods, and handicrafts. The primary agricultural products are barley, citrus fruits, olives, and livestock. The currency for Morocco is the dirham.

LITERACY ACTIVITIES

Lifestyles in Morocco

RL.K.1, RL.1.1, RL.2.1, RL.3.1

Ask the students what they know about Morocco. List responses on chart paper. Use Google Earth or a map, globe, or an app to locate Morocco. Discuss the styles of clothes, what the villages look like, and specifically the life of people in Morocco. What types of things are sold? Who is in the village? What are the roles of men, women, and children? Then tell the students that the story they are about to read or listen to is about Mustafa, a young boy who is able to learn many languages.

Knowing languages other than your own can broaden one's perspective in life. Have the students make connections to the story. Ask students if they know other languages like Mustafa. Does this story remind them of anything in another book they have read? Have they read or had books read to them in another language? Write the words on chart paper as the students dictate them to you.

Diverse Languages I

L.2.5, L.3.5

Place students in groups of three. Tell students that each group will practice and learn diverse languages like Mustafa. Assign each group *two to three* diverse words to learn. For example, have one group practice the number one in English, Spanish, and Japanese (one, uno, itchie). Once students have accomplished this task, the teacher-led recording may begin.

Have students practice the following prompt: I can say "one" another way—"uno." OR I can say "one" many ways—"uno" or "itchie." Provide student access to many languages with the app Free Translator. This translator has over forty languages including Czech, Danish, Dutch, English, French, German, Italian, Japanese, Korean, Polish, Portuguese, Russian, and Spanish.

Diverse Languages II

L.2.5, L.3.5

To help students become familiar with diverse languages, have the students return to the story and identify the different ways roosters crow "cock-a-doodle-doo" around the world. Have students make a word web with different languages using "Something to Crow About" (see figure 2.3).

SOMETHING TO CROW ABOUT!

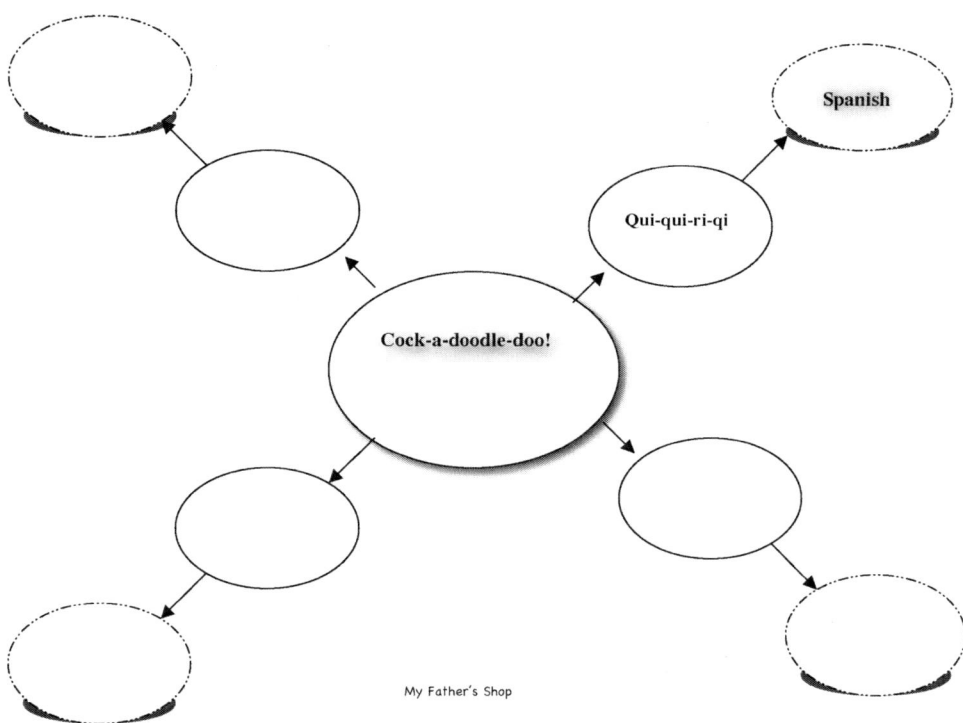

Figure 2.3. Something to Crow About

Students work in small groups to research and create additional word webs by writing different languages from around the world. Students will begin this activity by placing their chosen/target word in the middle of the word web, then write the word in a different language. The next step is to identify the name of the country in which each word originates.

Fictional Writing

W.2.3, W.3.3, SL.2.5, SL.3.5

Compare the shops in the United States and in Morocco. What is different/ similar? Have the students write about which country they would open a shop in and why. Then have students create a digital story (appendix B) using GarageBand, iMovie, PowerPoint slideshow, or Windows Movie Maker depicting items that would be found in their shop. Be sure to add text, images, voice, and music to the presentation.

Spotlight Morocco

SL.2.5, SL.3.5

Have students produce an episode on Morocco for the class weekly, bi-weekly, or monthly radio show. Student groups will create MP3 (Audacity) or MP4 (video) digital files to (1) report a glimpse of Morocco's geography, history, and culture; (2) share a summary of Moroccan books read; or (3) share information about Moroccan authors.

SENEGAL
Sofie and the City **by Karima Grant (2006)**
Grade Levels: K–3
Themes: Friendship, Moving, Feelings

Summary:

The story is about a young girl named Sofie, who recently moved to New York from the country of Senegal, West Africa. She is unhappy with the move but becomes happy when she finds a new friend. Montecalvo's use of acrylic illustrations depicts Sofie's feeling throughout the story.

Country Information:

The Republic of Senegal is a country of rolling plains and warm tropics. The country's rainy season starts in May and ends in November, when the hot, dry season begins. The southern portion of Senegal has an abundance of vegetation, which sharply contrasts with the very dry northern areas.

The population of Senegal is diverse with a majority of Senegalese divided between three main ethnic groups: Wolof, Pular, and Serer. The official language of Senegal is French, but the traditional languages of Wolof, Pulaar, Serer, and others are also spoken by many Senegalese. The majority of Senegalese are Muslim, but small populations of Christians and traditional religion worshippers live in the country. The average life expectancy of Senegal is fifty-six years.

Senegal is a republic with a three-branch system of government (executive, legislative, and judicial) similar to the United States. Children in Senegal attend primary school at higher rates than they do in later grades (75.8 percent versus the 11 percent attendance in secondary school).

The average literacy rate is 59.1 percent. Senegal's natural resources include fish, peanuts, iron, gold, and cotton. Agricultural products include peanuts, rice, vegetables, fruits, and flowers. Industry in Senegal focuses on mining, fishing, construction, and manufactured products.

LITERACY ACTIVITIES

Life in Senegal and New York City

RL.K.1. RL.1.1, RL.2.1, RL.3.1

Ask the students what they know about Senegal, West Africa. Record their responses on chart paper. Use Google Earth, a map, a globe, or an app to locate Senegal. Discuss the landscape, weather, and vegetation. Discuss the ethnic groups and languages. Then ask students what they know about New York City.

Both places can be compared using a Venn diagram (appendix A). Two interlocking circles can be drawn to represent each place. The left circle's area that does not touch the right and the right circle's area that does not touch the left contain statements that show how they are different. The area where the two circles overlap contains statements that show similarities in both places.

Friendship

SL.K.1

Ask students to tell you something about their friend. Ask students to draw a picture of their friend and then tell you his/her name and something they like to do with their friend. For example, "My friend's name is _____. I like to (play/sing/eat popcorn with him/her)."

Writing a Friendship Poem

W.1.1, W.2.1, W.3.1

Sofie, the young girl in the story, was unhappy about moving to a new country until she found a new friend. Have the students think and talk about the word "friendship" and what it means to them. Students will write to inform their audience about a friend. Probe students' thinking by asking the following questions:

- What makes a good friend?
- What do you like best about your friends?
- What do you do to make your friends happy?
- What do your friends do to make you happy?

Write their responses on chart paper. Then have the students write a poem about a friend, as shown in figure 2.4. An acrostic poem is a good way to write about a person. Have the students write their friend's name in a top-to-bottom position: the first letter of each line will spell out his/her name.

Drew B AFRICA

Writing a Friendship Poem

Create an acrostic poem
using your friend's name.
Write each letter in his/her name in a
top-to-bottom position. Use as many lines as needed.

Every day, she is always happy.
Living a good life
It can always be a great day with her
Zipping through activities
Always being amazing
Being spectacular in everything
Even when something goes rong
The most magnifesent athleat
Happy as can be!

Activity 2: Sofie and the City

Figure 2.4. Drew's Poem

Descriptive Word Bank

L.1.5, L.2.5, L.3.5

To help students become familiar with descriptive words, bring in wordless picture books and/or pictures from magazines. Have students describe what is happening in the picture by focusing on the descriptive qualities in the picture. Have students brainstorm words that describe size, shape, color, etc. Then have students make digital flashcards with the app Simple Flash Card Maker.

Descriptive Writings

W.1.3, W.2.3, W.3.3

After the story has been read and discussed, tell the students they will write a descriptive story. They will use "juicy words" that give the reader vivid details to help create vivid pictures. They will share their story with another student in an identified partner classroom in the building.

The storyteller combines narrative with digital content such as images, sound, and video to make a three- to five-minute movie. Ask the students what they will tell their friend about their real or pretend transition. What would they say in describing their new home? New school? New friends?

Spotlight Senegal

SL.2.5, SL.3.5

Have students produce an episode on Senegal for the class weekly, bi-weekly, or monthly radio show. Student groups will create MP3 (Audacity) or MP4 (video) digital files to (1) report a glimpse of Senegal's geography, history, and culture and (2) share the summary of Senegalese book(s) read.

SOUTH AFRICA
Mandela: From the Life of a South African Statesman
by Floyd Cooper (1996)
Grade Levels: K–3
Themes: Family, Village, Courage, Apartheid, Injustice

Summary:
This book is a biography of Nelson Mandela focusing mainly on where he came from and how his character developed throughout his life. It talks about his happy childhood, his stubborn personality, and his desire to stand up for what he believes in, while also portraying him as a strong-minded student and ultimately a leader.

Country Information:
The Republic of South Africa is located on the southernmost tip of Africa. This country is a little bit less than twice the size of Texas and has plateaus and mountains in its interior. Its climate is similar to California's, with warm weather for the majority of the year. There are several official languages in South Africa, including Afrikaans and English. South Africans are predominantly Christian, but Hinduism, Islam, Judaism, and traditional African religions are also seen practiced.

In recent years, South Africa has been a site of great political and social upheaval. For a time, South Africans were legally divided into four ethnic groups: black, white, colored (mixed), and Asian. South Africans still struggle with these ethnic distinctions and this can be seen in their schools, which were previously segregated.

Because South Africa is an area of high AIDS and HIV rates, the life expectancy for men and women is drastically lower than seen in the United States. Women, on average, can be expected to live until the age of forty-one, and men may only live to forty-three.

The South African government is a parliamentary democracy. The president and parliament share equal powers in the government. However, the South African government is a three-branch system. South Africa is known for being the only country to produce fuel from coal. Other industries present in South African are mining, manufacturing, information technology, agro-processing, textiles, and minerals.

LITERACY ACTIVITIES

Mandela's Extraordinary Life

RL.K.1. RL.1.1, RL.2.1, RL.3.1

Students will engage in the B-K-W-L-Q (Allen 2004) to build background knowledge and to enhance comprehension. This strategy is a form of KWL (Ogle 1986) that includes two added features: the "B" column is used for building background knowledge, while the "Q" column is used to record further questions. KWL stands for "What do you know? What do you want to know? And what have you learned?"

After the teacher and the students explore information about Mandela, the teacher reads a selection from the book as the students use the "B" column to write information about him. Ask the students what they know about Mandela. Record their responses on chart paper. Then ask them what they would like to know about Mandela and record this information in the "W" column. After the students read the entire book silently, the teacher records information in the "L" column. Following a lively discussion about Mandela, ask the students if there are further questions.

Mandela Sentence Starter

W.K.8, W.1.8, W.2.8, W.3.8

After reading stories about Mandela, ask students to tell you something they remember about him. Then let them know they will create an eBook using iBooks Author (an interactive book editor) or a podcast about Mandela. Use the following sentence starter to help structure their ideas. Finally, have them dictate what they have learned about him using an iPod. They will say, "I learned that Mandela _____."

Writing a Bio Poem

W.K.2, W.1.2, W.2.2, W.3.2

Students will compose a bio poem while focusing on Mandela's characteristics. Tell students that when writing the bio poem, they will describe him in eleven lines using the specific formula in figure 2.5. Provide students with access to Google docs to complete this task.

Nelson Mandala's Bio-Poem

(First name)–
(Four adjectives that describe the person)
Son or Daughter of (your parents names)
Lover of (three different things that the person loves)
Who feels (three different feelings and when or where they are felt)
Who gives (three different things the person gives)
Who fears (three different fears the person has)
Who would like to see (three different things the person would like to see)
Who lives (a brief description of where the person lives)
–(last name)

Example:

Nelson
Brave, extraordinary, strong-minded, leader
Son of

Figure 2.5. Bio-Poem

Read-Cover-Remember-Retell

RL.K.2, RL.1.2, RL.2.2, RL.3.2

Students will use the Read-Cover-Remember-Retell (Hoyt 1999) strategy to help gain a better understanding of the text. During Read-Cover-Remember-Retell, students will stop frequently to think about meaning making. To illustrate the Read-Cover-Remember-Retell strategy, let students *Read* (aloud or silently) only as much as their hand can cover, making sure they understand the big ideas and remember important facts. Then they *Cover* the words with their hand and *Remember* what they read in their own words (looking back is acceptable).

Reporting a News Story

RL.1.7, RL.2.7, RL.3.7, W.1.8, W.2.8, W.3.8

Tell students to pretend that Nelson Mandela will be visiting the city. Have students imagine they are reporters for the Astoria Park Elementary Radio (APER) station. After a brief interview with Mandela, they will gather interesting facts from him as well as from multiple print and digital sources to write their news story.

Students will begin by thinking of a headline for their report. For example, "Mandela, The Man, The Legend" or "Mandela Visits Ohio." In the report, students will talk about his life—for example, what has happened, who has been involved, when and where events took place, and how or why the events took place. Students will work in small groups to create a digital video using iMovie or Windows Movie Maker.

Spotlight South Africa

SL.2.5, SL.3.5

Have students produce an episode on South Africa for the class weekly, bi-weekly, or monthly radio show. Student groups will create MP3 (Audacity) or MP4 (video) digital files to (1) report a glimpse of South Africa's geography, history, and culture and (2) share the summary of South African book(s) read.

RELATED APPS AND WEB RESOURCES

Apps for Africa

- *Ansel and Clair's Adventure in Africa:* A top game app for kids to learn and explore the wonders of Africa via a fun, highly interactive, and educational game play.
- *Figurative Language:* Students read a short sentence, then practice their understanding of figurative language by choosing the best explanation out of three that fits each literary term.
- *Hello South Africa:* Eleven languages of South Africa translation app.
- *Sleepover in Africa at Amani's Graduation:* We like how the app allows children to learn about another country and culture via an interactive and engaging story.

WEBSITES

East Africa

For Teachers:

All Africa

http://allafrica.com/
A source for current news stories in Africa that might lead to classroom discussion (suitable for older kids and teachers).

http://www.africa.mrdonn.org/
Mr. Donn's webpage on the geography, history, art, and culture of Africa. Includes information, games, lesson plans, and even clipart.

Time for Kids

http://www.timeforkids.com/around-the-world
http://www.timeforkids.com/TFK/teachers/aw/wr/main/
0,28132,590829,00.html
A site for teachers, including worksheets and graphic organizers.

African Crafts

http://www.africancrafts.com/educs.php
Links to information on how African cloth is made and Kente paper weaving craft for kids (second grade).

African Kids

http://www.ibike.org/library/africakids.htm
This webpage includes information for kids on children's games, books, photos, and links to other resources.

History for
Kids Africa

http://www.historyforkids.org/learn/africa/
A good resource for the history of Africa for older kids (aimed at middle schoolers), but may serve grades 3 and 4 as well.

Morocco

For Teachers:

Children's Songs
Morocco

http://www.mamalisa.com/?t=ec&p=1212&c=168
Children's songs from Morocco, including the Happy Birthday song, some MP3s, etc.

Morocco
Presentations

http://countries.pppst.com/morocco.html
Website includes links to a variety of sites for teachers and children, including folklore and food. Several PowerPoint presentations are available, as are sites specifically for kids.

Teacher Link
Resources

http://teacherlink.ed.usu.edu/tlresources/units/byrnes-africa/densag/index.html
Compares a Moroccan folktale with a European one. Targeted to second graders.

Lesson Plans
Morocco

http://cmes.arizona.edu/outreach/lessons#M
Includes a variety of lesson plans for different ages, all concentrated on North Africa. The site is sponsored by the University of Arizona's Center for Middle Eastern Studies.

For Students:

Video of Morocco

http://www.youtube.com/watch?v=XSdILqrE-oo
Video of a Morocco visit narrated by a child.

Senegal

For Teachers:

http://www.cultureconnections.org/
A teaching resource specifically on Senegal and West Africa, this site sells artifact boxes from the region and could give teachers idea of things to include as discussion artifacts.

http://africa.unc.edu/outreach/resources/teaching_tolerance .pdf
Challenges stereotypes about the African continent.

http://news.bbc.co.uk/2/hi/africa/country_profiles/1064496.stm
This site provides a concise overview of Senegal, its history, and other important information.

http://www.arts-are-essential.org/saproject06/lesson_plans/lp _elem_AfricanMasks.pdf
A lesson plan for making Senegalese-style masks and a discussion of how they are used.

http://www.arts-are-essential.org/saproject06/lesson_plans/lp _elem_Mudcloth.pdf
This site is targeted to middle school students but the lesson plan could be adapted to younger students as well.

http://www.mnh.si.edu/africanvoices/mudcloth/html/index_text .html?showhtml
Discusses the creation of mudcloth.

http://www.gowestafrica.org/kids/lessons/Senegal.pdf
What life is like in Senegal lesson plans, including improvised toys (helping kids make "rag football"). Includes worksheets and games.

For Students:

 http://mag.amazing-kids.org/2010/09/30/ak-adventures-oct
-2010/
  Olivia Pineda shares her month-long experience in Senegal.

South Africa

For Teachers:

 http://www.shirleys-preschool-activities.com/childrens-litera
ture-lesson-plans-south-africa.html
  Includes information about additional books set in South
Africa that can be tied into this unit. Also includes samples of
language (common words like Mom, Dad, teacher, etc.).

For Students:

 http://kids.nationalgeographic.com/kids/places/find/south-africa/
  Pictures, tidbits, and a map, more appropriate for older kids.

3

ASIA (NORTH)

CHINA
My Chinatown: One Year in Poems **by Kim Mak (2002)**
Grade Levels: K–3
Themes: Moving, Tradition, Seasons

Summary:

A small Chinese boy has recently moved to Chinatown in New York and misses the things that he left behind, "a country, a language, a grandmother, and [his] animal chess game." Though it is not the same as being in Hong Kong, many things happen in Chinatown as the season changes that remind him of his home country. Mak's photo-like beautiful illustrations and his simple poems tell a story of a small boy who lives in a small city within a city, a place called Chinatown.

Information on Hong Kong:

The mountainous island of Hong Kong has a history of good governance. In 1842 Hong Kong was a part of the British Empire. In 1997 the British gave control over the island to the People's Republic of China. However, because of various laws, the island was allotted fifty years to make the gradual transition from British to Chinese rule. Until this occurs, Hong Kong is currently an independent local democratic government.

Hong Kong's climate allows for seasonal changes similar to regions in the United States: winter months are cool, and the spring to fall months are rainy and warm. The majority of the population is ethnically Chinese, and Cantonese and English (the official languages) are widely spoken. Almost half the population practices local religions in one form or another, with about 10 percent of those indicating that they are Christian.

The life expectancy of the average person in Hong Kong exceeds the average for the United States, with men living to seventy-nine and women to eighty-five. Hong Kongers enjoy high literacy rates, though a gap does exist between men and women (97 percent for men and 90 percent for women). Hong Kong's economy supports manufacturing industries with an emphasis on textiles and electronics.

LITERACY ACTIVITIES

Two Chinese Cultures

RL.K.I. RL.1.1, RL.2.1, RL.3.1, RL.K.10, RL.1.10, RL.2.10, RL.3.10

Ask the students what they know about Hong Kong. What do they know about Chinatown? Then point out the locations of these two places on a globe, map, or on the Internet. Tell students the boy in the story moved from Hong Kong to Chinatown in the United States.

Have students listen to the poems to learn about the two Chinese cultures. Then have students work in small groups to discuss things the boy saw in Chinatown that were similar to the things in Hong Kong. What things were different? List responses on chart paper or a SmartBoard.

Writing a Letter

W.K.6, W.1.6, W.2.6, W.3.6

Sometimes moving to a new place can make you homesick. Especially when you long to be with family and friends back home. Have students brainstorm ideas about what they would say to the small Chinese boy about the United States so he won't feel as homesick.

Have students record their ideas on the graphic organizer Great Things About the United States (appendix A). Students think and write about what he can learn and experience in the United States that he may not have been able to do in China. Have the students discuss foods, important people, and places that make the United States a special country to live in. Then ask students to work in pairs to write a letter of encouragement to the little boy using a digital device.

Word Knowledge

L.K.5, L.1.5, L.2.5, L.3.5

The small Chinese boy says, "When we left Hong Kong, we had to pack quickly," and many things got left behind. If you go home today and your family tells you that you are moving to a different country tomorrow, what would you pack in your luggage?

Have the students make a list of the things they would take with them. Students will demonstrate an understanding of these items by using the words in a sentence. In each sentence, they will explain how each item relates to their life. Have the students write their lists of words and sentences as in figure 3.1.

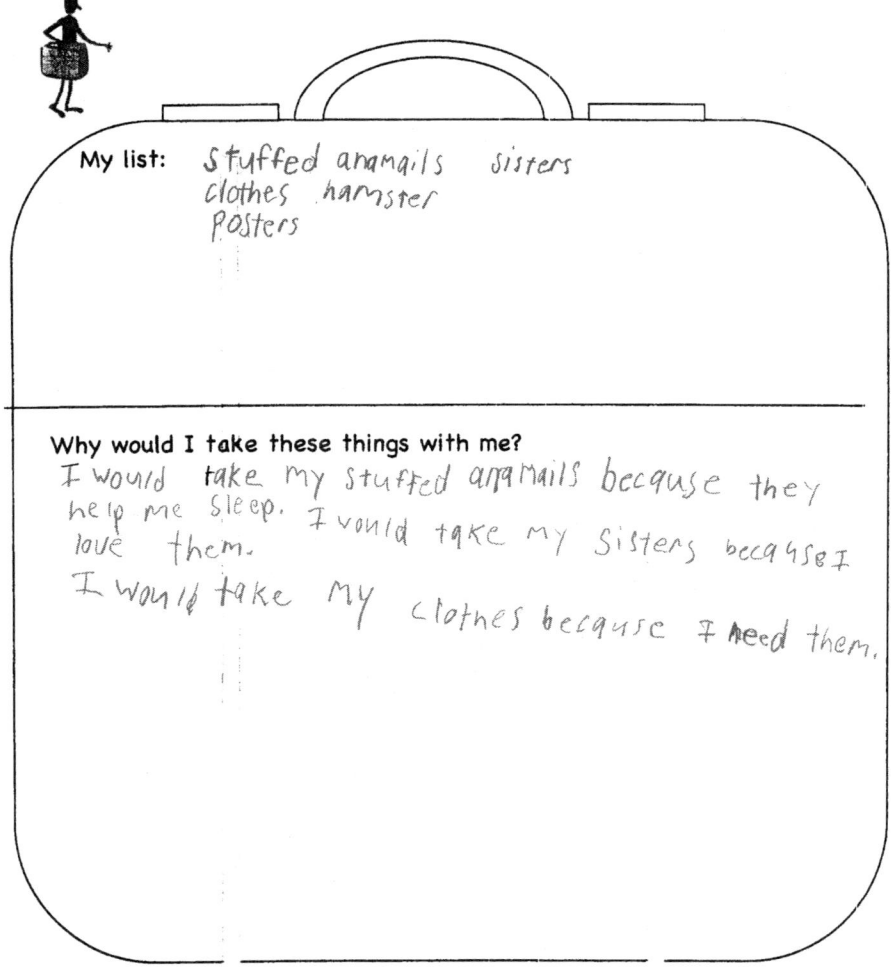

Jordyn

What would I take with me?

Inside the suitcase, make a list of things you will take with you if you had only one day to pack. Then write why you decided to take the things on your list with you.

My list: Stuffed anamails   sisters
            clothes   hamster
            posters

Why would I take these things with me?

I would take my stuffed anamails because they help me sleep. I would take my sisters because I love them.

I would take my clothes because I need them.

Activity 3: My Chinatown

Figure 3.1.   Word Knowledge

Writing Sentences

W.K.6, W.1.6, W.2.6, W.3.6

Once the students have completed the activity "What would I take with me?" have students create a PowerPoint slideshow depicting items they would pack and type sentences explaining the significance of these items in their lives. Use narration to add voice to the presentation.

Spotlight Hong Kong

SL.2.5, SL.3.5

Have students produce an episode on Hong Kong for the class weekly, biweekly, or monthly radio show. Student groups will create MP3 (Audacity) or MP4 (video) digital files to (1) report a glimpse of Hong Kong's geography, history, and culture and (2) share the summary of Chinese book(s) read.

A Song for Ba by Paul Yee (2004)
Grade Levels: K–3
Themes: Changes, Tradition, Family Values, Generation

Summary:

Wei Lim's father and grandfather both sing in the Chinese opera in Chinatown. Wei wants to learn how to sing, but his father wants him to get an education rather than learn opera, a tradition that may die. Wei secretly learns from his grandfather until he leaves Wei to go back to China.

When Wei's father is forced to play a high-toned female role due to the lack of audience in Chinese opera, Wei starts singing, remembering what he had learned from his grandfather, and tries to help his struggling father. Wang's colorful painting portrays a family passing down the tradition from one generation to the next.

Country Information:

The People's Republic of China is a country of great biodiversity. Its mostly mountainous land areas include regions of tropical and subarctic climates. China is the fourth-largest country in the world and can claim the tallest mountain peak on record, Mount Everest. China is home to several languages and dialects. The most commonly spoken is Standard Chinese, also called Mandarin.

Despite the country being officially atheist, there are a few small populations of Chinese who practice Taoism, Christianity, and Islam. The average life expectancy of the Chinese is a little lower than in the United States, with women living to an average of seventy-five and men to seventy-one. Literacy rates in China are also lower than in the United States, with only 90.9 percent of the population over fifteen years of age able to read.

The People's Republic of China is a communist state, which means the government owns everything and distributes resources to its citizens based on need. The current president is Xi Jinping. The laws of the government are based on a mixture of Soviet doctrine and their own civil law system. Chinese cultural traditions include the performance arts, such as the Chinese opera. Today the Chinese opera is making a comeback in the country after harsh restrictions placed on it by the government finally ended.

LITERACY ACTIVITIES

Making Predictions

RL.K.1, RL.1.1, RL.2.1, RL.3.1

In the story, Wei's father, Ba, tells him that things have changed between his grandfather's and the younger generations. Discuss with the students how things have changed from their grandparents' generation to now. List responses. Before reading the story, ask students to predict why they think fewer people are now watching Chinese opera. What do they think would happen if the number of people who watch the opera decreases to the point that they have to shut down the business? What will happen to the people in the business and to Chinese culture and tradition?

Read the story and have the students discuss in small groups how to bring people back to the Chinese opera. Then have students create an advertisement using Glogster (www.edu.glogster.com), an interactive poster or webpage. Students begin this activity by copying responses onto My Plan to Bring People Back to the Chinese Opera (appendix A).

Synonyms

L.K.4, L.1.4, L.2.4, L.3.4

Wei's grandfather felt tradition was as important as education. Tell students the importance of keeping the tradition of one's culture and getting an education. Create a T-chart on an interactive whiteboard and ask students to brainstorm words for the tradition column, then have students write a list of synonyms in the education column for each word to show the benefits of both tradition and education.

For example, if the teacher provides the word *necessary* in the tradition column, the students may write *essential* or *important* in the education column. To practice using synonyms, give students access to the apps Apples and Pairs or Find Synonyms. Lexipedia (www.lexipedia.com), an online dictionary and thesaurus, can also be provided to students for searching, identifying, and adding synonyms to the education column.

Story Retelling

RL.K.2, RL.1.2, RL.2.2, RL.3.2, RL.K.3, RL.1.3, RL.2.3, RL.3.3

After students have read or listened to the story, allow them to individually tell you what happened at the beginning, middle, and end of story. If students stop retelling the story, use the following prompts below for probing:

- Tell me more about . . . (main characters in the story, where the story takes place).
- What else can you tell me about Wei? Ba? Grandfather?
- What did Grandfather teach Wei to do?
- What made Wei recognize his father on opening night?

My Opera Report

W.K.7, W.1.7, W.2.7, W.3.7, W.K.8, W.1.8, W.2.8, W.3.8

Ask how many students have seen an opera. How is it different from musicals? What is the history behind it? Introduce students to the free online news source for current events called Dogo News (www.dogonews.com).

Each article includes a series of comprehension questions and a critical thinking challenge question for engaging in argumentation of the text. Then have the students research the topic "opera" in small groups. After deepening their understanding about opera, have students write then use Audacity to report the new information they have learned. Teachers can also create a short opera with the class and use Audacity to record it.

Spotlight Chinatown

SL.2.5, SL.3.5

Have students produce an episode on Chinatown for the class weekly, biweekly, or monthly radio show. Student groups will create MP3 (Audacity) or

MP4 (video) digital files to (1) report a glimpse of Chinatown's geography, history, and culture and (2) share the summary of a Chinese book(s) read.

JAPAN
Kamishibai Man by Allen Say (2005)
Grade Levels: K–3
Themes: Tradition, Storytelling, Change

Summary:

Jiichan is a Kamishibai man, a Japanese storyteller who moves around on a bike with a big box on the back that has stories inside. The world has changed due to advanced technology, and he lost his little audiences who used to come and listen to his stories and buy candies.

After many years, Jiichan decides to go back and tell one more story—his story. As he reads his last passage, he is surprised by the audience that had gathered; there they were, the children that he used to tell stories to were listening to his story again as a grownups. Say's touching illustrations capture the heart of Jiichan's passion for storytelling and the world that is constantly changing.

Country Information:

Japan is an island country with none of its borders touching any other land. The climate is moderate and has seasonal changes. Japan is known for its many unique cultural traditions. Japan is home to the geisha and samurai traditions romanticized in recent movies. Other traditions include the tea ceremony (also found in China), where the drinking of tea is a highly practiced ritual intended to show respect to the host and guests.

For the written traditions, haiku and tanka were developed in Japan. These short poem forms follow specific line lengths and use simple words and phrases to convey larger meanings. Storytelling also has its place in traditional Japanese culture. Comedic storytelling is known as *rakugo*, and stories that are more serious minded are called *kôdan*. Unlike Jiichan, many performers practice their art in theaters known as the *yosé*.

LITERACY ACTIVITIES

Comparing the Past and Present

RL.K.6, RL.1.6, RL.2.6, RL.3.6, RL.K.9, RL.1.9, RL.2.9, RL.3.9

Ask the students what they know about Japan. Then point out the location on a globe, map, or on the Internet. Tell students that this story focuses on changes that have occurred in the world due to the development of technology. Have students brainstorm things they have today that their parents or grandparents may not have had when they were children (for example, computer games).

Discuss what life would be like if the students were to go back fifty years, and describe what they would do. Then, as a group, students complete a past and present comparison chart (see figure 3.2) after gathering the information from the text with prior knowledge and experience using two categories: communication and transportation (for example, writing a letter versus sending email, riding bicycles versus driving cars).

Past and Present

PAST	PRESENT
Communication:	Communication:
Transportation:	Transportation:

Figure 3.2.   Past and Present

Recognizing Compound Words

L.2.4

Before reading the story, tell students they will be detectives in search of compound words in the story. This activity can be used before, during, or after reading. The teacher will model using "Think Aloud" as he/she searches and scans the book for compound words then writes them on chart paper or the SmartBoard.

Another way to enhance students' knowledge of compound words is to provide them access to a vocabulary website (www.vocabulary.co.il) or the app

Make a Compound Word. Finally, students work in small groups to identify and share other compound words in the story (for example, hillside, Grandpa, Grandma, himself, afternoon, rooftops, storyteller, etc.).

Point of View

RI.K.6, RI.1.6, RI.2.6, RI.3.6

Have the students interview a grandparent, parent, or any older adult to find out how things were in the past and how things have changed from their viewpoint. The following day, have students come back together as a class and revisit the story and the past and present comparison chart they previously made. If there were new findings, these will be added to the chart.

Descriptive Writing

W.K.1, W.1.1, W.2.1, W.3.1, W.K.3, W.1.3, W.2.3, W.3.3

Based on the chart Past and Present, have students brainstorm ideas and discuss what their future may look like. Will technology be even more advanced? If so, what will it look like? In addition to thinking about what the world will look like in the future, have students use juicy descriptive words as they write a class story (with the teacher's assistance) using the SmartBoard or iBooks Author. In the story they will describe what it may be like twenty years from now. Be sure the story includes a beginning, middle, and end.

Spotlight Japan

SL.2.5, SL.3.5

Have students produce an episode on Japan for the class weekly, bi-weekly, or monthly radio show. Student groups will create MP3 (Audacity) or MP4 (video) digital files to (1) report a glimpse of Japan's geography, history, and culture and (2) share the summary of a Japanese book(s) read.

Suki's Kimono by Chieru Uegaki (2003)
Grade Levels: K–3
Themes: First Day of School, Friends, Self-Confidence, Courage

Summary:
On the first day of school, Suki wears a kimono that her grandmother gave her as a gift, but her sisters laugh at her, saying that Suki should wear something new or

cool instead. Even when Suki gets stared and chuckled at, she proudly shows her kimono and talks with her classmates about her grandmother's visit from Japan. Jorisch's lively watercolors express Suki's excitement to share her summer experience and the story teaches the readers to be proud of their culture and that true friendship does not come from how you look.

Country Information:

Japan is a country that consists of a chain of islands just off the coast of China. The total landmass of the islands is comparable to the size of California. Japan has a distinct culture with a history of isolationism that lasted until the mid-nineteenth century.

After Japan became integrated in global affairs, the country adopted several Western society–inspired progressive reforms. This included the disbanding of the traditional feudal system and instituting laws that would transform Japan into a constitutional monarchy with the emperor serving as the chief of state. Japan has a rich traditional culture in which festivals occur regularly and traditional forms of dress, like the kimono, are still worn at formal occasions.

The Japanese have higher life expectancies than recorded for the United States, with women on average living to eighty-five and men to seventy-eight. Because of their educational reforms, 99 percent of the population is literate, with no distinction between men and women.

Shintoism and Buddhism are the most widely practiced religions, with a significant portion of the population following both. Because Japan does not have many natural resources, it depends largely on manufactured goods with transport equipment and motor vehicles as its primary exports. To this day, Japan is the only country that had an atomic bomb used against it in war.

LITERACY ACTIVITIES

Text-to-Self Connections

RL.K.I. RL.I.I, RL.2.I, RL.3.I, RL.K.3. RL.I.3, RL.2.3, RL.3.3

Students will read about or listen to Suki's first day of school. Have students make text-to-self connections (Fountas and Pinnell 2001) as they think about their first day of school. Ask students what they would do if the teacher wore something that was "different" because it was special to him/her.

Ask students if they ever experience wearing something "different" to school. Tell students that Suki wore something special to school. However, her sisters told her she shouldn't wear it because everyone would think she's weird, they would laugh, and no one would play with her. Have students read or listen carefully to find out what she wore, what it looked like, and why she wore it. After reading or hearing the story, ask students what they would do if they were Suki.

Significant Selections

RL.K.7, RL.1.7, RL.2.7, RL.3.7

Throughout the story, different events occur and the characters in the story react to Suki differently. As readers read a story, they bring in various ideas, and how one person reacts to the book may be different from a classmate who is sitting right next to him/her.

Have the students choose significant selections from the story and write what they were thinking as the events occurred. Have students write responses using Good Readers Think (appendix A), then compare them with a friend and see how he or she was thinking about their own responses.

Suki's Word Challenge

L.K.4, L.1.4, L.2.4, L.3.4

Choose target words from the story such as *kimono, geta, obachan, obi, school, somen, taiko*. A copy of the word knowledge chart (figure 3.3) will be given to students to place a check in the box that shows evidence of their level of word knowledge (Allen 1999; Nagy 1988; Stahl 1999). The levels include *have heard it, have seen it, know it*. For example, if a student has heard the word but has not seen it or doesn't know it, then have him/her place a check in the box next to the words "has heard it."

Suki's Word Challenge

Directions: Look at the pre-selected words. Say each word and place a check in the box to identify your level of word knowledge [have heard it, have seen it, know it.] Then write what you think the word means. Finally, use a dictionary or other sources to write what the word really means.
*You may write additional words during or after reading the story.

Words	I have heard it	I have seen it	I know it	I think it means	It really means
geta					
kimono					
school					
somen					
taiko					

Figure 3.3.   Suki's Word Challenge

Story Writing

RL.K.2, RL.1.2, RL.2.2, RL.3.2, W.K.3, W.1.3, W.2.3, W.3.3

Ask the students if they have ever worn special clothes and for what purpose. Have the students talk about what they learned about Suki's kimono. Discuss why it is shaped as it is, when people wear it, and what it is like to wear it (if you have access to a kimono, have the students try it on). Next, provide students access to the app Tools 4 Students to assist them in organizing prewriting ideas. Then have the students design a kimono using the template in appendix A and write about what they learned from reading *Suki's Kimono*. Students may work individually or in pairs.

Spotlight Favorite Clothes

SL.2.5, SL.3.5

Have students produce an episode on Japan for the class weekly, bi-weekly, or monthly radio show. Student groups will create MP3 (Audacity) or MP4 (video) digital files to (1) tell about a time when they wanted to wear something out of the ordinary to school and (2) share a glimpse of that favorite clothing and explain what made it special but out of the ordinary.

KOREA
Halmoni's Day **by Edna Bercaw (2000)**
Grade Levels: 1–3
Themes: Adaptation, Grandparents, Immigration, Languages

Summary:
Jennifer, a Korean American girl, is worried when her grandmother visits from South Korea. Her school's Grandparents' Day was the next day and the fact that her grandmother wore a traditional Korean dress and spoke no English made her nervous that she will be embarrassed in front of all of her friends. Hunt's realistic illustration portrays the understandings across generations and cultures.

Country Information:
The Republic of Korea controls a land area just slightly smaller than the state of Indiana. The climate is moderate but has been known to experience occasional typhoons. The population of South Korea is remarkable because it is relatively nondiverse. With the exception of a small Chinese population, South Koreans are mostly of the same ethnic and linguistic group. However, diversity is enjoyed in its religious sector with Catholicism, Protestantism, Buddhism, and other traditional religions practiced.

The government of South Korea is a republic with elected officials including a president (who appoints a prime minister) and legislators. The majority of the population is literate (98 percent) and education is mandatory for the first nine years. The average life expectancy is also similar to that in the United States. At one point in their histories, North Korea and South Korea were one country, but civil war tore them apart. Despite this, South Korea has a thriving economy. It boasts a strong industry in electronics and telecommunications.

LITERACY ACTIVITIES

Making Connections with Jennifer

RI.K.3, RI.1.3

Tell students that the story they are about to read or listen to takes place in South Korea. Use the Internet, an app, a map, or a globe to locate South Korea. Jennifer, the girl in this story, is worried about something. Have students discuss their experience of being worried or something that would make them feel worried. List the responses of the students.

Ask if anyone has or knows of someone who has a grandparent from another country. Jennifer was worried when her grandmother came from Korea. Tell students to read or listen to find out what about Jennifer's grandmother made her worry. Have the students think about a time when they thought someone in their family might embarrass them in front of their friends.

Cultural Detective

RL.K.1, RL.1.1, RL.2.1, RL.3.1

Have the students be culture detectives. Ask them to write things they found in the book that shows the Korean culture. What did Halmoni wear? What did she say? What did Jennifer do? Have the students discuss other things they saw in this book from Korea. What kind of food was eaten, clothes were worn, shelter was presented, and language was spoken? Then have the students compare and contrast things they found in the story with their own culture using Be a Culture Detective in appendix A.

Analyzing Jennifer's Feelings

RL.2.5, RL.3.5

Have students discuss how Jennifer's feelings changed throughout the book and find out how they changed before and after the visit to school for Grandparents' Day. Think about why her feelings changed and write responses as shown in figure 3.4.

Figure 3.4.   **Analyzing Feelings**

History of My Grandparents

RL.K.1, RL.1.1, RL.2.1, RL.3.1, W.K.3, W.1.3, W.2.3, W.3.3

Tell the students that grandparents play a very important role in every family. Have students create a digital story of their grandparent(s). First, ask the students to engage in family research by interviewing their grandparents. Tell students to ask leading questions such as "Where were you born?" or "What was it like going to school?" or "What are your favorite books?" or "How did you meet grandpa/grandma?" Next, have them write a narrative and bring it to class for creating their digital story. Students will share their digital stories using Audacity, a free audio tool, or Animoto, used for creating stories with audio.

Spotlight Korea

SL.2.5, SL.3.5

Have students produce an episode on Korea for the class weekly, bi-weekly, or monthly radio show. In this episode, student groups will create segments using MP3 (Audacity) or MP4 (video) digital files to (1) report a glimpse of Korea's geography, history, and culture and (2) share the summary of a Korean book(s) read.

RELATED APPS AND WEB RESOURCES

Apps for Asia (North)

- *Monki Home:* Another great way for young children to not only practice vocabulary acquisition in three different languages but also practice some of the familiar routines they see at home.
- *Popplet:* A productivity app that also works as a mind-mapping tool. Use the app to begin structuring the writing process.
- *SentenceBuilder:* An app that helps children learn to build grammatically correct sentences about a given picture.
- *Apples and Pairs:* This app allows your students to practice synonyms or antonyms by matching like or unlike words.
- *Hiragana Nazori/*ひらがななぞり: For each kana, you can listen to the pronunciation and watch an animation of the stroke order (you can adjust the speed too).
- *Miaomiao's Chinese New Year:* Throughout the app, children must help Miaomiao and Doudou by completing fun and intuitive mini games that advance the story. With explanations of cultural traditions and twenty easy-to-learn Mandarin vocabulary words, every page is full of Chinese New Year–themed words and fun interactions waiting to be discovered.

WEBSITES

China

For Teachers:

Lesson Plans China

http://www.shirleys-preschool-activities.com/preschool-lesson-plan-china.html

Includes lesson plans and books related to China, how to make a Chinese lantern (for early childhood/preschool), book suggestions, information about Chinese food, etc.

Chinese Language

http://www.timeforkids.com/destination/china

Website on the Chinese language (including pronunciation audio files) and history. Older kids may be able to navigate this site alone.

Chinese History

http://china.mrdonn.org/

Chinese history and culture, information about people, places, festivals, culture, crafts, and philosophy. Older kids (grades 2 to 3) may be able to navigate this site without teacher assistance.

Chinese Opera

http://www.firstpalette.com/Craft_themes/World/Chinese_Opera_Mask/Chinese_Opera_Mask.html

Chinese opera mask craft for kids, with printable templates included.

For Students:

National Geographic— North China

http://kids.nationalgeographic.com/kids/places/find/china/

Geography and a video about northern China becoming more of a desert. Includes information and links relating to the Chinese New Year, the Terra Cotta army, the Olympics, panda bears, etc.

History for Kids

http://www.historyforkids.org/learn/china/

Includes information pages about Chinese history, science development, food, and more.

Japan

For Teachers:

*Lesson Plans—
Hinamatsuri Day*

http://www.brighthub.com/education/early-childhood/arti cles/36365.aspx

A lesson plan relating to Hinamatsuri Day ("Girl's Day" Holiday).

Storytelling

http://www.planetesme.com/storytelling.html

A site for teachers about teaching kids to tell stories.

*Lesson Plans—
Native American*

http://www.atozteacherstuff.com/pages/438.shtml

Lesson plan relating to the Native American tradition of a storytelling stick.

For Students:

Japanese Facts

http://web-japan.org/kidsweb/

Facts and information about Japanese culture, including Manga, spooky stories, and folk legends.

Korea

For Teachers:

Korean Songs

http://www.mamalisa.com/?p=972&t=ec&c=140
Korean songs for children, some with MP3 sound files (with English lyric translations).

Lesson Plans—
My Family

http://www.atozteacherstuff.com/pages/370.shtml
"My Family and Me" lesson plan in which students create a personal book about their family.

For Students:

National
Geographic

http://kids.nationalgeographic.com/explore/countries/south
-korea/
Photos and facts on South Korea.

4

ASIA (SOUTH)

BANGLADESH
Basket of Bangles: How a Business Begins by Ginger Howard (2002)
Grade Levels: 2–3
Themes: Business, Bank, Market, Women of Bangladesh, Natural Disaster

Summary:

Sufiya walked around begging for rice from her neighbors every day, but one day she gets an idea about starting a business. She gathers four other friends in order to borrow money from the bank and starts selling bangles. She makes money, buys some food, pays interest to the bank, and saves some money for emergencies. Noll's colorful illustrations capture the women of Bangladesh and its culture.

Country Information:

The People's Republic of Bangladesh is a country of hills and flowing rivers. The country experiences warm weather year round and experiences annual summer torrential rains known as monsoons. Bangladeshis are an almost homogeneous population with 98 percent of the population Bengali. The dominant religion in Bangladesh is Islam, but the Hindu religion also has a significant presence. The official languages of Bangladesh are Bangla and English.

Many of the people in Bangladesh are involved with agricultural work. Because of the abundance of natural water sources, Bangladesh is an ideal place to grow rice. The country also produces wheat, tobacco, various spices, and oilseeds. Its industries produce paper newsprint, cement, garments, and chemical fertilizer.

Despite these agricultural opportunities, about half the country lives below the poverty line. Also, half the population age fifteen and up are not fluent readers.

This is not helped by the fact that the Parliamentary Democratic Bangladeshi government is struggling with political upheaval. Because of the political climate, the ability to focus on school and work reforms becomes much more difficult.

LITERACY ACTIVITIES

Exploring Bangladesh

RL.2.1, RL.3.1

Before reading the story, have students work in pairs to conduct research on Bangladesh. Ask students to identify the location, physical characteristics, climate, currency, etc. Use the Internet or an app, map, or globe to locate Bangladesh. Discuss with the students similarities and differences between Bangladesh and the United States. Record responses on chart paper or a SmartBoard.

Story Sequencing

RL.2.5, RL.3.5

Have students work with a partner. Ask them to take a few minutes to recall the events in the story in order. Then give each pair a sheet of lined paper that has been previously placed in a plastic sheet protector and wipe-off markers. Students can also use digital apps such as Notability or N+OTES for keeping notes. Students use a different color marker each time they add a new event of the story. Once they have written several events (number determined by the classroom teacher), have students share with the class.

Star Synonyms

L.2.5, L.3.5

The ladies in the story went to Taslima to learn the rules of the bank. She told them they should follow four principles of the bank: discipline, unity, courage, and hard work. List examples of how each principle was portrayed in the book. Then divide the students into four business groups and assign each a principle of the bank.

Have them write a list of synonyms to describe their principle. Then write an example of how their star principle could be met using one of The Four Principles (see appendix A for blank samples). To practice using synonyms, give students access to the app Apples and Pairs or Find Synonyms. Lexipedia (www

.lexipedia.com), an online dictionary and thesaurus, can also be provided to students for searching, identifying, and adding synonyms to their star principle.

Making a Business Plan

RL.2.1, RL.3.1

This book tells about how the characters needed to make economic decisions such as planning and saving for starting a business. In small groups, have the students come up with a plan they would use to start a business at the market in Bangladesh.

Ask them to think about their principles, resources they will need to purchase, how much money they will have to borrow from the bank, and how much they plan to save in case of an emergency using Steps to Starting Our Own Business in appendix A. Provide students with the app Business Plan Creator.

Spotlight Bangladesh

SL.2.5, SL.3.5

Have students produce an episode on Bangladesh for the class weekly, bi-weekly, or monthly radio show. In this episode, student groups will create segments using MP3 (Audacity) or MP4 (video) digital files to (1) report a glimpse of Bangladesh's geography, history, and culture and (2) share the summary of Bangladeshi book(s) read.

INDIA
***Monsoon* by Uma Krishnawami (2003)**
Grades Levels: K–3
Themes: Rainy Season, Summer, Family, Market

Summary:
In India the rainy season "monsoon" is an important part of the country's agriculture and culture. In *Monsoon*, a young girl anticipates the arrival of the monsoon season. The book follows her discussions with family members about what the monsoon used to be like. She also finds herself wondering what will happen if the monsoon never comes at all. *Monsoon* is beautifully illustrated and a treat to look at over and over again.

Country Information:
India is a country of great diversity. With the world's second-largest population (just slightly behind China), India is home to many different kinds of people and

beliefs. There is some debate about the official number of ethnic groups in India. The majority of the country practices Hinduism, but significant pockets of the population follow Islam, Christianity, and other established local religions. There are twenty-one official languages, with Hindi being the foremost spoken language. English is not an official language but is used in matters of business.

India is a federal republic, meaning that the central government enjoys more power than individual jurisdictions. This is different than the United States, where the central government shares equal power with the individual states. India used to be under the control of the British crown until January 26, 1950, when war-weary Britain granted them independence. India has several important natural resources such as coal, iron, diamonds, titanium ore, and crude oil. Its industries produce textiles, steel machinery, fertilizers, and computer software.

LITERACY ACTIVITIES

Learning About India

RL.K.1, RL.1.1, RL.2.1, RL.3.1

Tell students that the setting of the book they are about to read or listen to is in India. Use the Internet or an app, map, or globe to locate India. Assess students' background knowledge and/or experience about the monsoon rain in India by using a KWL (know, want to know, learned) chart (Ogle 1986). Engage students in this activity before and after they read or listen to the story.

As the students brainstorm what they know about monsoons, have students record their responses or list responses in the first column on chart paper or a SmartBoard. Then have students generate questions of what they want to know about monsoons. However, if students' background is limited, stop at this point to broaden their understanding through pictures, videos, discussions, etc. Once the story is read, record what they have learned in the last column. Figure 4.1 is an example of the KWL chart.

Taj Jamar Boxie JR.

Monsoon Rain in India
KWL Chart

what I *K*now	what I *W*ant to know	what I *L*earned
−Make floods − it's in india	−when does it flood? −why does it flood? −what makes it flood? −I wonder if the floods are dangerous! −how long does it rain.	−Sometimes monsoons are good and bad. −The monsoons help the crops grow. −sometimes monsoons are bad because people can be homeless.

Activity 1: Monsoon

Figure 4.1. KWL_Taj

Miniature Monsoon

RL.K.1, RL.1.1, RL.2.1, RL.3.1, W.K.3, W.1.3, W.2.3, W.3.3

Have students create a miniature version of the story *Monsoon* by writing or dictating one-sentence summaries. When summarizing, students will recall and arrange the important events in a logical sequence. The following prompts may be used to guide their summaries (Oczkus 2003): *this page was about, the most important idea is, why do I think that, etc.*

After reading the story, give each student several passages from the book. Guide the students to choose the most important information and write or dictate it in their own words. Then have the students use Summarizing *Monsoon* in appendix A to complete the summaries.

Compound Collection

L.2.4

Students work in pairs to collect compound words from the story. Give each pair a set of blank index cards, two different color markers, and a plastic resealable bag. Then students revisit the story and begin searching for compound words. Because these words are made of two smaller words, the students will write each word using a different color marker.

Next, they will place the word in the resealable bag and continue searching for more words. Finally, have each pair choose one compound word from their collection and share the first part of with the class. Ask the class to come up with the second part of the word. For example: *seashore, sunshine, peacock, billboards, etc.* Teachers can also provide students access to a vocabulary website (www.vocabulary.co.il) or the app Make a Compound Word.

Persuasive Writing

W.2.I, W.3.I

Pretend you are a forecaster and it is monsoon season. People are wondering if the monsoon rains will come soon. They also wonder how much, how fast, and how hard will it rain. Some even wonder if they will ever come. Prepare the weather information for the evening news by writing a persuasive paragraph.

What will you say to persuade the people whether or not the monsoon rains are coming? Students will work in small groups to create a digital video for broadcasting the information. Provide students with video production tools such as Jing, Screencast-O-Matic, or the app GoView.

Spotlight India

SL.2.5, SL.3.5

Have students produce an episode on India for the class weekly, bi-weekly, or monthly radio show. In this episode, student groups will create segments using MP3 (Audacity) or MP4 (video) digital files to (1) report a glimpse of India's geography, history, and culture and (2) share the summary of book(s) from India.

INDONESIA
Rice Is Life **by Rita Gelman (2000)**
Grade Levels: K–3
Themes: Animals, Cycle of Rice, Rice, Farmers

Summary:
    Rice is eaten for breakfast, lunch, and dinner by the people on the island of Bali in the country of Indonesia. Gelman's poetic structure and Choi's oil paintings portray the importance of rice for the people in Bali and how it grows as the animals take part in the life cycle of rice.

Country Information:

Lying in Southeastern Asia between two oceans is the archipelago of the Republic of Indonesia. This large, tropical land mass is surrounded by several islands. The Indonesian population is composed mostly of the Javanese, Sundanese, and Madurese ethnic groups. The majority of Indonesians are Muslim with small populations practicing Christianity and Hinduism. The official language is Bahasa Indonesia, but English and Dutch can also be heard.

Education is mandatory for all children until the ninth grade, and enrollment is high. However, after the ninth grade enrollment is reduced by little less than half with only 57 percent of children taking the equivalent of high school courses. Literacy rates are lower than in the United States, with a noticeable discrepancy between men and women.

The government of Indonesia is an independent republic with a constitution that focuses on five state-sanctioned principles: monotheism, humanitarianism, national unity, representative democracy, and social justice. Indonesia's natural resources include oil, silver, and tin. Its agricultural industry produces rice, rubber, timber, and coffee.

LITERACY ACTIVITIES

Learning About Rice

RL.K.I, RL.I.I, RL.2.I, RL.3.I

Ask students what they know about Bali, which is located on an island in Indonesia. Use the Internet or an app, map, Google Earth, or globe to locate Bali, Indonesia. Tell students that rice is one of the main crops in Bali. Ask students if they know of someone who grows rice. Then ask students if they eat rice, when they eat it, how often to they eat it, and the ways in which it is cooked. Do they add anything to it once it is served? Record students' responses on chart paper or a SmartBoard.

Writing in Sequence

W.K.3, W.I.3, W.2.3, W.3.3

After reading the story, discuss with the students about how farmers grow rice in Bali. Ask the students to share how it is grown. What is the environment like? Then have the students create a small booklet (see figure 4.2) on how they grow rice. Tell students to use sequence words like *first, then, next.* Other sequence words are *second, third, before, after,* etc. Finally, tell students that the story must be written in sequential order with a beginning, middle, and end. Provide students with the app Tools 4 Students to organize their thoughts and ideas.

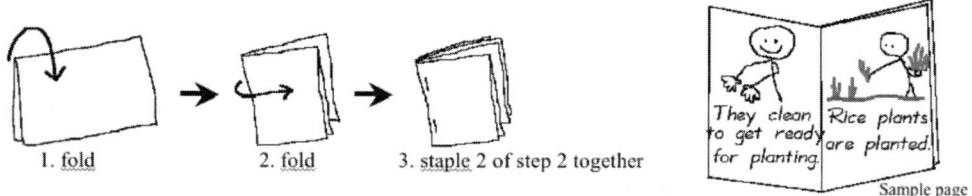

1. fold   2. fold   3. staple 2 of step 2 together

They clean to get ready for planting. Rice plants are planted.

Sample page

Figure 4.2. Sequencing

Vocabulary Harvest

L.K.4, L.I.4, L.2.4, L.3.4

As the rice grows, the book *Rice Is Life* tells a story about the various animals and insects that live near or in the rice field. Have the students revisit the story and select action verbs that are used to describe the animals and insects. Then ask students to sort words accordingly (Bear, Invernizzi, Templeton, and Johnston 2004).

A sample sort is shown in figure 4.3. To help guide students' sorting, tell them to write the name of the chosen animal and/or insect on the top row (see sample). Next, have the students cut apart their list of words or write each word on cards for sorting words into piles.

Dragonfly	Bat	Mice
fluttering	looking	squeaking
dancing	eating	
	flapping	

Figure 4.3. Vocabulary Harvest

Expository Writing

W.K.2, W.1.2, W.2.2, W.3.2

Rice Is Life focuses on how rice is cultivated in Bali, Indonesia. Tell the students to research and explain how rice is grown in other parts of the world. Have students begin by making a statement about rice in a particular place. Then add three details to support the main idea and the conclusion. Students can work individually or in small groups as they record the story using Audacity or other digital production tools.

Spotlight Indonesia

SL.2.5, SL.3.5

Have students produce an episode on Indonesia for the class weekly, bi-weekly, or monthly radio show. In this episode, student groups will create segments using MP3 (Audacity) or MP4 (video) digital files to (1) report a glimpse of Indonesia's geography, history, and culture and (2) share the summary of book(s) from Indonesia.

AFGHANISTAN
Four Feet, Two Sandals by Karen Williams (2007)
Grade Levels: K–3
Themes: Friendship, Sharing, Refugee Camp, Hope

Summary:
Even in the worst situations, compassion and goodwill can blossom. Such is the case with Lina and Feroza, two Afghani girls living in a refugee camp in Peshawar on the Afghanistan-Pakistan border. Each girl shares their stories of grief and hope over the simple act of sharing one pair of sandals. The shoes begin to symbolize the bond they share with each other by wearing the sandals on alternate days or by each wearing one sandal.

Karen Williams explains the desperate situation of people and children living in refugee camps around the world in her Author's Note. For classrooms that wish to explore modern-day issues, this book confirms human strength of spirit while highlighting the fact that the world can be an uncertain place.

Country Information:
In 2004 the country adopted a new constitution and became the Islamic Republic of Afghanistan. During that time, Hamid Karzai became the first president and was later reelected in 2009. However, in 2014 Ashraf Ghani became president and Abdullah Abdullah served as chief executive officer.

Afghanistan is a completely landlocked country and because it is desert country there are few water resources. Afghanistan has a history of mixture of different cultures, and as a result several different ethnic groups are represented. The main ones are Pashtun, Tajik, Hazara, Uzbek, and Turkmen. Many different languages are also spoken, reflecting the many different dialects of ethnic groups. However, Dari and Pashto are most commonly heard.

Perhaps the greatest unifier in the country is its cultural association with Islam. Formal education is not yet fully enforced in the country, with only 36 percent of Afghani children attending. Of this percent, males make the majority. Even so, only 52 percent of males and 24.2 percent of females are literate.

LITERACY ACTIVITIES

Book Box

RL.K.I, RL.I.I, RL.2.I, RL.3.I

Show students the cover of the book. Tell students this story takes place in Afghanistan. Then point out the location of the Middle East using the Internet or an app, map, Google Earth, or globe. Next, place the following items in a box: one flip-flop, a small pail, a clear baggie of sand, a map focused on the Middle Eastern countries, and a tent.

Tell students that they will be detectives and must try to make predictions about what the story will be about based on the clues in the box. Show students the objects one at a time, and have students list each item and then individually write their prediction in their writer's notebook. Allow students time to share their predictions.

Checking Predictions

RL.K.I, RL.I.I, RL.2.I, RL.3.I, W.K.I, W.I.I, W.2.I, W.3.I

Students will monitor their predictions throughout the text. Begin by reading through the passage that states, "Suddenly the girl turned, taking the matching sandal with her" (Williams 2007). Ask students to modify their predictions as necessary. Allow each student to share his or her predictions with a partner. Continue reading to the section in which Lina and Feroza decide to share the flip-flops.

Have students check predictions and make new predictions. Continue reading through the section that describes when Feroza's grandmother tells Lina that her mother's name is on the list. Have students write their predictions and discuss with a chosen partner.

Finish the story and allow time for students to go back and review their predictions and outcomes. Allow time for discussion about the predictions. End with students writing their predictions of whether Lina and Feroza will be together again in America.

Writing a Postcard

W.K.5, W.1.5, W.2.5, W.3.5

Provide each student with a half-sheet of the postcard template (appendix A). Students will think about Lina in America, where she might live, and what she might be doing. Then students will take on the identity of Lina and write a short postcard to Feroza discussing what has happened and where she has visited so far in America. Students need to draw a corresponding picture on the reverse side of the postcard depicting where Lina currently is in America or a specific place she has traveled to thus far.

Letter Writing

RL.K.6, RL.1.6, RL.2.6, RL.3.6, W.K.3, W.1.3, W.2.3, W.3.3

Students will be placed into pairs and take on the roles of either Lina or Feroza. Students will write a letter (see figure 4.4) from the point of view of Lina in America and one from the point of view of Feroza. Provide students access to the online letter generator in Readwritethink (www.readwritethink .org/files/resources/interactives/letter_generator/). After completing the writing process for each letter, they will record their letters using Audacity or other digital recording tools. At the end of the lesson allow each group to share their podcast with the class.

May 17 2015

Dear Feroza,

I am having a good time
in America. I am going
to a new school named Blue
waters Elementary. I made some
new friends named Jamie and Jessica

P.S. My friend has the same
Pair of sandles we shared.

from: Lina

Figure 4.4.   Letter Writing

Spotlight Afghanistan

SL.2.5, SL.3.5

Have students produce an episode on Afghanistan for the class weekly, bi-weekly, or monthly radio show. Student groups will create MP3 (Audacity) or MP4 (video) digital files to (1) report a glimpse of Afghanistan's geography, history, and culture and (2) share the summary of book(s) from Afghanistan.

RELATED APPS AND WEB RESOURCES

Apps for Asia (South)

- *Kids Planet Discovery:* A colorful and engaging new app that has something for every child, whether they're fascinated with puzzles, animals, dolls, or music. With the whole world as its focus, there is a lot of interesting material to cover.
- *Dress Up Party:* Dress Up Party is a colorful and creative way to learn a little bit about the cultures of India as players dress characters in traditional colors and styles.
- *ACFlash Indonesian Flash Cards:* Fun Indonesian flash cards. Learn over 1,000 words with the help of these colorful and interactive vocabulary flash cards. Great for everyone from casual travelers to serious students.
- *Apples and Pairs:* This app allows your students to practice synonyms or antonyms by matching like or unlike words
- *Story Builder:* A multipurpose app designed to teach story structure. In the process, students learn sentence structure, sequencing, and inferencing.

WEBSITES

Bangladesh

For Teachers:

Virtual Bangladesh

http://www.virtualbangladesh.com/bd_contents.html
Information and background on Bangladesh, many images, information on history, geography, culture, etc.

Resource for Kids

http://www.ducksters.com/geography/country.php?country=Bangladesh
A resource for kids with a brief history, geography facts and map, and fun facts.

India

For Teachers:

Activity Village

http://www.activityvillage.co.uk/india_for_kids.htm
   Collection of activities for kids that teach about Indian culture.

PBS-India

http://www.pbs.org/thestoryofindia/teachers/lessons/PBS
   Videos about several different aspects of India culture and life.

For Students:

National
Geographic-India

http://kids.nationalgeographic.com/kids/places/find/india/
   Photos, facts, and videos on India.

Time for
Kids-Hindi

http://www.timeforkids.com/destination/india
   A website with information and activities for kids, including
a historical timeline and a page for practicing words in Hindi.

Indonesia

For Teachers:

Mrdonn-Indonesia

http://countries.mrdonn.org/indonesia.html
   Resources for activities involving Indonesia.

http://www.proteacher.com/redirect.php?goto=5490
Activities involving wild animals in Indonesia.

Proteacher
Indonesia

For Students:

http://www.sciencekids.co.nz/sciencefacts/countries/indonesia
.html
Fun facts and general information about Indonesia for kids.

Science Kids
Indonesia

Afghanistan

For Teachers:

http://www.public.asu.edu/~apnilsen/afghanistan4kids/index2
.html
Stories and activities about Afghanistan culture.

Afghanistan
Culture

http://www.proteacher.com/redirect.php?goto=556
Printable flag to color.

Flag

http://countries.mrdonn.org/afghanistan.html
Resources for lesson plans about Afghanistan.

Lesson Plan
Afghanistan

For Students:

*National
Geographic
Afghanistan*

http://kids.nationalgeographic.com/kids/places/find/afghanistan/
Photos, facts, and videos on Afghanistan.

5

CARIBBEAN

HAITI
***Circles of Hope* by Karen Williams (2005)**
Grade Levels: K–3
Themes: Family, Planting Trees, Hope

Summary:

Facile, a young Haitian boy, attempts to plant a tree in honor of his new baby sister, just as his father planted a tree for him when he was born. After many attempts, he finally finds a solution. Saport's use of charcoal and pastel creates a warm feeling that embraces the family bond that Karen conveys with her words.

Country Information:

The Republic of Haiti shares the island of Hispaniola alongside the Dominican Republic. The country of Haiti has many beautiful coastal areas and mountains, which makes the country popular for tourism. Ninety-five percent of Haitians are descendants of Africans brought to the island by Europeans for labor. The majority of Haitians are Christian, though local religions (such as vodou) are also practiced by some. The official languages of Haiti are French and Creole (a mixture of French, Spanish, English, and tribal languages).

Haiti has a young population with a median age of eighteen. This is partially due to the prevalence of AIDS and because an extremely high unemployment rate means most people cannot afford basic necessities. The average life expectancy is fifty-six for women and fifty-two for men. Literacy rates are also low, and education is only mandatory for six years. Haiti has a largely service-based economy but it also has a large agricultural base, mostly in coffee, mangoes, sugarcane, and cacao.

LITERACY ACTIVITIES

Learning About Haiti

RL.K.I, RL.I.I, RL.2.I, RL.3.I

Tell students that this story takes place in Haiti. Use the Internet, or an app, map, Google Earth, or globe to locate Haiti. Have the students look back at the story and see what kind of environment Facile is trying to plant the tree in. Keep in mind the tree Facile's father had planted for him when he was born "was the only tree on the whole dusty mountaintop."

Why is it so hard to plant trees in his environment? What do seeds need to grow, and what was missing? Have students use What Does It Take for a Plant to Grow? (see appendix A) to record their responses. The free app Leafsnap can be utilized to help explore and identify trees in the surrounding area.

Predicting and Checking Predictions

RL.K.I, RL.I.I, RL.2.I, RL.3.I

After completing the activity, review what seeds need to grow (air, water, nutrients, living space, and light). Then have the students grow their own seeds. Students will place four lima bean seeds on a wet paper towel in a resealable bag and tape them on the window.

Have them predict what will happen to the seeds and how long it will take for them to sprout. Draw and write their predictions in their science journals. In addition, make a big chart in the classroom on how the seeds are growing.

Materials:

- sandwich bags
- lima bean seeds
- paper towels
- scotch tape
- science journal

Sequencing

RL.K.I, RL.I.I, RL.2.I, RL.3.I, RL.K.7, RL.I.7, RL.2.7, RL.3.7

Discuss with the students about different ways one can honor a family member. In small groups, have the students choose what they would plant if a new family member joined their family and research how to plant the flower of their choice and how to take care of it. As shown in Libby's recipe in figure 5.1, have students write their own recipe. (Use http://www.urbanext.uiuc.edu/firstgarden/planning/dictionary/flowers/index.html for reference.)

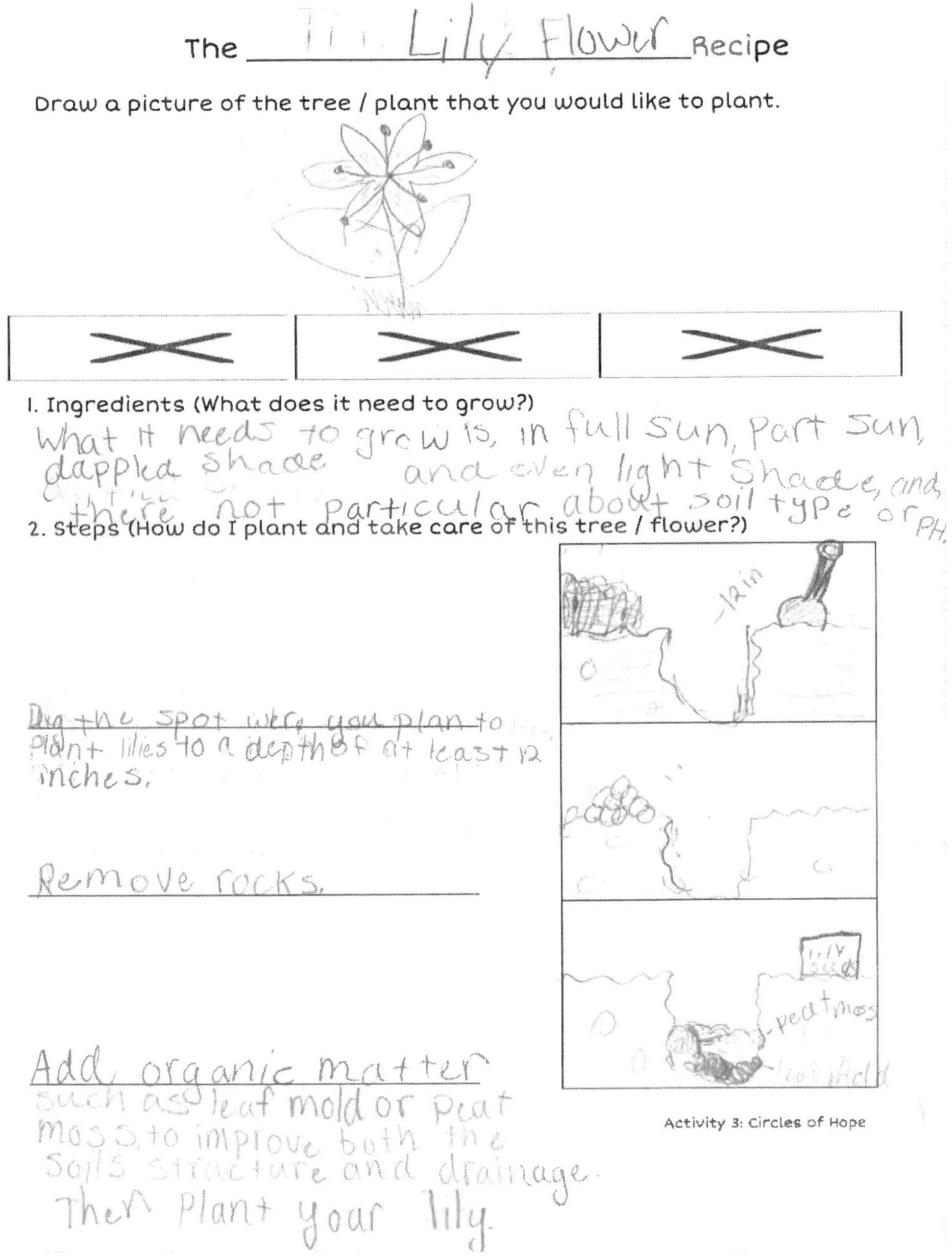
The Lily Flower Recipe
Draw a picture of the tree / plant that you would like to plant.
1. Ingredients (What does it need to grow?)
What it needs to grow is, in full sun, Part sun, dappled shade and even light shade, and there not particular about soil type or PH.
2. Steps (How do I plant and take care of this tree / flower?)
Dig the spot were you plan to plant lilies to a depth of at least 12 inches.
Remove rocks.
Add organic matter such as leaf mold or peat moss, to improve both the soils structure and drainage. Then plant your lily.
rain
lily seed
peat moss
Activity 3: Circles of Hope

Figure 5.1. Sequencing

Broadcasting a Home and Garden Show

RL.1.7, RL.2.7, RL.3.7, W.1.8, W.2.8, W.3.8

Pretend you are the host of a new Home and Garden show. Every evening you tell your audience how to grow and take the best care of plants. Students will form small groups to compose a message, then broadcast the show using GarageBand, iMovie, or Windows Movie Maker. What would be the name of your show? What type of plants would you tell your audience about?

Spotlight Haiti

SL.2.5, SL.3.5

Have students produce an episode on Haiti for the class weekly, bi-weekly, or monthly radio show. In this episode, student groups will create segments using MP3 (Audacity) or MP4 (video) digital files to (1) report a glimpse of Haiti's geography, history, and culture and (2) share the summary of Haitian book(s) read.

JAMAICA
Under the Breadfruit Tree by Monica Gunning (1998)
Grade Levels: 2–3
Themes: Family, Friends, Dialect

Summary:

Through use of descriptive poetry, Monica Gunning spins the story of a Jamaican family and their friends. The characters have their own stories and their own personalities; Grandma is proud and hardworking, while Aunt Sara is a silly gossip.

Each poem told through the point of view of a young girl highlights small or large events in the lives of the characters. The stories are often sweet, sometimes funny, but they never ignore the concerns of life that are common to all humankind.

Country Information:

The island of Jamaica is located just off the coast of Cuba. Because of its proximity to the equator, Jamaica enjoys tropical weather year round. The majority of Jamaicans are black, a legacy of the European trade routes. The official languages of Jamaica are English and English patois, which is like a Jamaican Creole (a mixture of languages).

Eighty percent of Jamaicans are religious, with the vast majority of the people believing in Christianity. Historically, Jamaica was valued for its sugarcane growing opportunities. Its top natural resources are sugarcane, bananas, and coffee.

Even though the government is independent, it is headed by the crown of England, currently Queen Elizabeth II. Because of this, the country is a constitutional parliamentary democracy with a separate prime minister and legislative branch. Currently Jamaica is undergoing a period of high unemployment and interest rates. Literacy rates are lower than seen in the United States, with women (at 92 percent) more likely than men (at 88 percent) to be literate.

LITERACY ACTIVITIES

Learning About Jamaica

RL.K.1, RL.1.1, RL.2.1, RL.3.1

Tell students that the poems they will listen to or read take place on the island of Jamaica. Use the Internet or an app, map, Google Earth, or globe to locate Jamaica.

Monica Gunning states that the languages and culture are a rich mixture of African, East Indian, Chinese, and European influences. Both English and Creole are spoken (p. 5). Allow students to experience the vocabulary of language using the glossary from the book *Under the Breadfruit Tree*. Record words and definitions using Audacity and have students listen to them during center time.

Mental Imagery

RL.K.1, RL.1.1, RL.2.1, RL.3.1, RL.K.7, RL.1.7, RL.2.7, RL.3.7

Discuss what it means to create mental images (Pressley 1995) while listening to or reading a selection. Instruct students to close their eyes and visualize what comes to their mind as they listen to the following selection from *Under the Breadfruit Tree*.

> Captain Bligh brought a treasure many suns ago to my island;
> trees bearing fruit, yellow-green and round, we eat like bread. (p. 7)

Tell students that the images they see will vary from person to person. Then ask the students to share what they saw and explain why. Chart responses on chart paper or a SmartBoard.

Author Study

RI.1.5, RI.2.5, RI.3.5, RI.K.6, RI.1.6, RI.2.6, RI.3.6

Have students work in small groups to engage in an author study. First, the students will learn about Monica Gunning by researching her personal and professional life using figure 5.2. Then have students compare two books by Monica Gunning using a Venn Diagram (appendix A) as they determine the similarities and differences of the books. Student will examine the author's style, illustration, and theme. Finally, students will select the book they prefer and explain why. Allow time for students to share their responses.

Biography Report Form/Organizer

Person's Name: _____

Birthdate:

_____

Hometown:

_____

Parents/Siblings:

_____

Date of death:

_____

What is this person famous for:

_____
_____
_____

Interesting facts about this person:

_____
_____
_____
_____

Four adjectives you would use to describe this person:

_____ _____ _____ _____

Quote from this person:

_____

What did you learn from researching this person?

_____
_____
_____
_____

If you could ask this person one question, what would it be?

_____
_____
_____

Figure 5.2.　Author Study

Writing and Recording Free Verse

W.K.2, W.1.2, W.2.2, W.3.2, W.K.5, W.1.5, W.2.5, W.3.5

Have students discover what a breadfruit tree is by presenting them with background information and pictures describing what it looks and tastes like using juicy adjectives. Use this reference for assistance: http://www.hort.purdue .edu/newcrop/morton/breadfruit.html#Description.

Finally, have students use free verse to add another selection to the poem. Have students record their free verse using Audacity.

Spotlight Jamaica

SL.2.5, SL.3.5

Have students produce an episode on Jamaica for the class weekly, bi-weekly, or monthly radio show. In this episode, student groups will create segments using MP3 (Audacity) or MP4 (video) digital files to (1) report a glimpse of Jamaica's geography, history, and culture and (2) share the summary of Jamaican book(s) read.

ST. THOMAS
Rata-Pata-Scata-Fata: A Caribbean Story by Phyllis Gershator (2005)
Grade Levels: K–3
Themes: Daydreaming, Chores, Family

Summary:
A gentle book about a young boy named Junjun who lives in St. Thomas. Because Junjun spends so much time daydreaming, he believes that uttering the words "rata-pata-scata-fata" will help him get his chores done.

City and Country Information:
The city of St. Thomas is located in a chain of islands known as the Virgin Islands. These islands are not part of an individual country; rather, they are protected territory under the United States. These islands are important to the United States because of the access to the Panama Canal granted to it for ships. St. Thomas in particular is appreciated for its deep natural harbor. Virgin Islanders enjoy status as being citizens of the United States, but because they are not a state, they cannot vote in presidential elections.

The majority of Virgin Islanders are black with smaller populations of whites and Asians. English is widely spoken, though about 17 percent of the population speaks Spanish Creole (a mixture of languages) with another 7 percent speaking French or French Creole. The Virgin Islands are exposed to powerful eastern winds that help keep the climate mild, despite their relative proximity to the equator. The islands' main sources of income include tourism, petroleum refining, pharmaceuticals, and electronics.

LITERACY ACTIVITIES

Learning About St. Thomas

RL.K.1, RL.1.1, RL.2.1, RL.3.1

Tell students that the story they will listen to or read takes place in St. Thomas, which is located in a chain of islands known as the Virgin Islands. Use the Internet or an app, map, Google Earth, or globe to locate St. Thomas. Tell students that Junjun liked to dream through the day.

Ask students if they remember dreaming during the day and ask them to tell what they were dreaming about. Show the students the cover of the book and ask them make predictions about the things they think Junjun might dream about in the story. Record student responses on chart paper or a SmartBoard. Then tell students to listen to or read the story to confirm their predictions.

"I Dream . . ." Poem

RL.K.1, RL.1.1, RL.2.1, RL.3.1, W.K.1, W.1.1, W.2.1, W.3.1

Tell student to recall things they may have dreamed about. Then students will use this information to write a class poem. Each student will write a line and begin it with the words, "I Dream . . ."

Plot Summary

RL.K.7, RL.1.7, RL.2.7, RL.3.7

Tell students that plot summary informs the reader of the sequence of events in the story. After students have listened to or read the story, have them make a fold-up book (see figure 5.3) or provide students with the app Animoto, used for creating stories with audio. Then write about what happened at the beginning, middle, and end of the story. Finally, ask students to draw a picture for each section of the story.

Plot Summary
Fold-up Book
(Cut then fold on dotted lines. Change the end of the story)

JuN JuN got fish

JuN JuN got a got

got

JunJun clees his room

R a ta
pa ta
sc at a
fata

Author: Dominic

*Change the end of the story.

Activity 3: Rata - Puta - Sata

Figure 5.3.   Plot Summary

Book Review

RL.K.1, RL.1.1, RL.2.1, RL.3.1, RL.3.6, SL.2.4, SL.3.4

Students will voice their opinions about the story. Begin by reviewing the process of examining a book. For example, tell students what you liked about the book and why, what you least liked about the book and why, etc. Next, provide each student with a copy of the book review template (appendix A) to complete a review of the story. Have students use a digital device to record their book review to share locally or globally.

Spotlight St. Thomas

SL.2.5, SL.3.5

Have students produce an episode on St. Thomas for the class weekly, bi-weekly, or monthly radio show. In this episode, student groups will create segments using MP3 (Audacity) or MP4 (video) digital files to (1) report a glimpse of St. Thomas's geography, history, and culture and (2) share the summary of St. Thomas book(s) read.

TRINIDAD AND TOBAGO
Fish for the Grand Lady by Colin Bootman (2006)
Grade Levels: K–3
Themes: Family, Hope, Courage, Dialect

Summary:
Derrick and his younger brother Colly decide that they are going fishing. They want to catch enough fish for their grandmother, "Grand Lady," for her to cook more than they could possibly eat in one day. Colin Bootman, the author, uses local expressions and grammar to make the characters' speech more representative of the country. The book comes with a short explanation of the words and phrases.

Country Information:
The Republic of Trinidad and Tobago consists of two islands located in the Caribbean. Trinidad and Tobago are the largest suppliers of petroleum and petroleum products in the Caribbean. They produce and export liquefied gas, methanol, and ammonia. These islands are also large producers of food and drink items.

The islands are 40 percent Indian and 38 percent African, and the rest of the population consists of mixed ethnic groups. Trinidadians and Tobagonians speak English as the official language, but Creole and a local version of Hindi called Caribbean Hindustani are also spoken. Roman Catholicism and Hinduism share similar percentages of population participation, with smaller groups of people practicing Islam and Protestant religions.

The government of Trinidad and Tobago is a parliamentary democracy. The president is elected with the full approval of both houses in the parliament (legislative branch). The prime minister is appointed by the president, each official sharing government duties and obligations.

LITERACY ACTIVITIES

Learning About Trinidad

RL.K.1, RL.1.1, RL.2.1, RL.3.1

Ask the students what they know about Trinidad. List responses on chart paper. Use the Internet, a map, or a globe to locate Trinidad. Tell students that the boys in this story wanted to do something special for their grandmother, Grand Lady. Ask students if they have ever wanted to give something special to a family member. If so, what was it? Why did they want to do it? Was it a special occasion? How did they go about planning it? Write responses on chart paper or a SmartBoard.

Story Problem

W.K.3, W.1.3, W.2.3, W.3.3

Model how to write about a story problem so students can see the complete process. Then have a volunteer read a precut story problem. Next, ask students these questions: (1) What is the important problem? (2) Why is it important?, and (3) How was the problem solved?

Repeat this process several times, then have students work in groups of four to six to write their own story. Give each group a different problem to solve. Tell students to begin their story with a problem, tell why it's important, and solve the problem, explaining how it will work out.

Feelings Chart

RL.K.1, RL.1.1, RL.2.1, RL.3.1, SL.K.1, SL.1.1, SL.2.1, SL.3.1

Begin by asking students if they can name any emotions or feeling words. Make a list of these words and discuss them with the students. Then have students engage in the activity "Guess How I Feel." During this activity, students

Serrena

Feelings Chart

Events	Derrick	Colly
Mrs. Wong gave them some hooks	Derrick is serious	smiling
By noon their snacks were gone.	SaD	unhappy
Colly fell down the muddy bank	Happy because they have fish	Happy wet and laughing

Fish for the Grand Lady

Figure 5.4. Feelings Chart

will identify a feeling that is being demonstrated by someone in the classroom. Then tell the students they will make inferences by analyzing the characters' behavior using a feelings chart (see figure 5.4). Students will reread or listen to the story and identify the character's feelings during a particular event in the story. Students will work in small groups or in pairs.

Descriptive Writing

W.K.1, W.1.1, W.2.1, W.3.1

Discuss character traits with the students. Then brainstorm and discuss additional traits. Write responses on chart paper. Then have students sort words according to characters in the story. Next, have students use the sorted words to write a descriptive paragraph about the character.

Spotlight Trinidad and Tobago

SL.2.5, SL.3.5

Have students produce an episode on Trinidad and Tobago for the class weekly, bi-weekly, or monthly radio show. In this episode, student groups will create segments using MP3 (Audacity) or MP4 (video) digital files to (1) report a glimpse of Trinidad's geography, history, and culture and (2) share the summary of book(s) from Trinidad.

RELATED APPS AND WEB RESOURCES

Apps for Caribbean Resources

- *Haiti Hub:* A complete system for learning Haitian Creole online.
- *Haiti Radio:* Free online Haitian music radio stations.
- *Haiti Untold:* Haiti Untold App is the official mobile application for the feature documentary "Haiti Untold," revealing the inside story since the devastation wrought by the Haiti earthquake of 2010.
- *Haiti Quick Facts:* Haiti Quick Facts is a high-quality, easy to use application featuring nearly 150 facts about its people, geography, government, weather, economy, politics, exports, communications, transportation, and military.
- *Jamaica Music and News Radio:* This is the number one radio and newspaper app for Jamaica.
- *Speaker Radio:* Create and share LIVE audio broadcasts on the go from your mobile device!

WEBSITES

Haiti

For Teachers:

Teaching
Citizenship

http://www.teachingcitizenship.org.uk/

According to the site, ACT is the professional subject association for those involved in citizenship education. Site has subjects for primary, secondary, and Post 16 students that have examples of how other teachers have delivered various aspects of citizenship across all phases of education. Information on the proposed new curriculum, curriculum for primary and secondary, modules, and other resources are available on this site.

Project Teach
Haiti

http://projectteachhaitiorg.fatcow.com/about-project-teach.html

Site is for teacher development at large in Haiti.

World Language

http://www.worldlanguage.com/Products/Creole/childrens books/Page1.htm

These are books in the Haitian language that can be purchased online for students according to their grade categories.

Haitian Educational Materials

http://www.haitianbookcentre.com/catalog/educational.pdf
Books, audio, games, software, and charts for sale.

Five Ways to Teach About Haiti

http://learning.blogs.nytimes.com/2010/01/14/5-ways-to-teach -about-haiti-right-now/

From Teaching & Learning in the *New York Times*. Participate in blog discussions with other teachers surrounding ways to teach about Haiti. Site has interactive features for students.

Scholastic

http://www.scholastic.com/browse/article.jsp?Id=3753349

Exhaustive site that includes resources and tools, strategies and ideas, books, and student activities.

Cultural Equity— Songs Children Sing in Haiti

http://www.culturalequity.org/rc/ce_rc_lessons_haitichildren songs.php

Site provides popular Haitian children's songs and lyrics with supporting questions and activities.

For Students:

Mama Lisa's World

http://www.mamalisa.com/?P=768&t=ec&c=114

Children's songs and rhymes in both Haitian Creole and English.

National
Geographic Kids

http://kids.nationalgeographic.com/explore/countrieshaiti/
Facts, photos, geography, and related content.

Jamaica

For Teachers:

MacMillan
Resources for
Jamaica

http://www.macmillan-caribbean.com/pages.aspx/resources_for
_jamaica/
Site provides information for teachers such as eBooks, exams, lesson plans, flashcards, and worksheets.

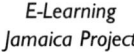

E-Learning
Jamaica Project

http://www.e-ljam.net/
Articles and links for presentations including digital photography and video, sound files, clip art, etc.

The Global
Exchange—
Jamaica

http://www.globalexchange.org/country/jamaica/background
A reference site for the background, economy, geography, Rastafarian Movement, and language of Jamaica.

BBC Jamaica
Lesson Plan

http://www.bbc.co.uk/northernireland/schools/4_11/cultureclub/
downloads/printouts/Jamaica-lesson-plan.pdf
A complete lesson plan that includes games, pictures, and other things to help with learning about Jamaica from a British perspective.

For Students:

Kid's Guide
to Jamaica

http://www.jamaicans.com/childsguide/
You will find lots to love here including the Jamaican National Anthem, Dr. Seuss read in patois, the traditional Happy Birthday song (Jamaican version), children in Jamaica, etc.

St. Thomas

For Teachers:

http://www.tolerance.org/lesson/talking-about-our-families
Lesson plans and activities for students in K–5 grades about families from different cultural backgrounds.

Teaching Tolerance—Talking about Our Families

http://www.britannica.com/ebchecked/topic/518303/Saint-Thomas
Extensive travel-type site profiling the U.S. Virgin Islands. Informs about the people, geography, government, etc.

Encyclopedia Britannica

http://computer.howstuffworks.com/internet/basics/how-to-podcast.htm
A general explanation of what a podcast is, what format to put podcasts in, and how to go about creating your own podcast. Contains background knowledge for teaching about podcasts and gives examples of working podcasts.

How Stuff Works: How to Create Your Own Podcast

For Students:

http://www.vinow.com/stthomas/History/
A visitor website that gives the background of St. Thomas and other Virgin Islands.

Vinow, St. Thomas: Virgin Islands Facts and History

http://kids.familytreemagazine.com/kids/default.asp
Kids can explore and create their own family tree to help understand how their family is structured.

Family Tree Kids! Making Family History Fun

6

EUROPE

BULGARIA
My Name Was Hussein by Hristo Kyuchukov (2004)
Grade Level: K–3
Themes: Adaptation, Grandparents, Immigration, Languages

Summary:

Hristo Kyuchukov writes a candid story about culture clash based on events experienced in his own life. As Islamic citizens of Bulgaria, Kyuchukov and his family were subject to the authority of their government and were expected to conform in much the same way that Hussein and his family do in the story.

The book explores the meaning of a name and the importance that tradition brings to individuals' understanding of themselves, their culture, and the world. The dream-like quality of the illustrations complements the eloquence of the writing.

Country Information:

The Republic of Bulgaria borders the Black Sea and is just south of Romania. Bulgaria's naturally cool climate makes for mild summers and winters with a lot of snow. Bulgaria is dominated by the Bulgarian ethnic group, but small Turkish and Roma populations do reside in the country. The majority of Bulgarians practice Bulgarian Orthodox, a branch of Catholicism, but some do practice Islam. The official language is Bulgarian.

A former communist country, Bulgaria has had a recent violent past socially and politically. Minorities, such as Muslims, were the target of government and civilian groups. However, under the communist government, women were given more rights and equality. Today Bulgaria is a parliamentary democracy. Some of the country's natural resources are bauxite, lead, zinc, timber, and coal.

LITERACY ACTIVITIES

Making Predictions

RL.K.1, RL.1.1, RL.2.1, RL.3.1

Tell students that the story they are about to read or listen to takes place in Bulgaria. Then point out the location of Bulgaria using Google Earth, a globe, an app, or a map. Ask students if they have ever been asked to give up something against their will. What was it? What did it feel like? Did they understand why this was happening to them? Then tell students that the story is about a boy and his family who were forced to give up something.

Next, take the students on a picture walk or have students preview the book. Have students use the Prediction and Confirming Chart (appendix A) to make predictions and record their responses about what they think will happen in the beginning, middle, and end of the story and why. Finally, have students display their chart in the classroom.

Practicing Phrase and Expressive Reading

RF.K.4, RF.1.4, RF.2.4, RF.3.4

Students need multiple reading opportunities to develop fluency. Provide each student with a copy of a selection from the text *My Name Was Hussein*. Then mark each selection in meaningful phrases or "chunks" (Rasinski 2003). Have students work in pairs as they practice reading the selection with appropriate phrasing.

Once students are confident reading the marked phrases, have them reread the selection to practice reading with expression. When students have successfully read the selection with phrasing and expression, have students practice reading the selection with unmarked phrases.

Say Something

SL.K.1, SL.1.1, SL.2.1, SL.3.1

During this interactive verbal activity, students stop and talk about the selection. Have students work in pairs for buddy reading (Harste, Woodward, and Burke 1984). Students may read a page before stopping to share their ideas or use stop points to guide their discussion.

Once they stop, they each share their thoughts with each other, then repeat the process. The following prompts can be used to enhance students' responses: say something to your buddy about *what you think might happen next, a particular character, the way the story began or ended, how a particular character feels, etc.*

Summarizing Strategy

RL.K.7, RL.1.7, RL.2.7, RL.3.7

Introduce students to the "Somebody Wanted But So Then" strategy (Macon, Bewell, and Vogt 1991), which will help them summarize the main events of the story. Have students read a selection of the story and discuss the following: *Somebody* (main character), *Wanted* (plot), *But* (problem), *So* (solution), and *Then* (resolution/outcome). After completing the column chart, students will read their summary statement. Figure 6.1 provides a sample of a blank column chart.

Name _____   Date _____

Book Title: _____

Author: _____

Someone... Who is the main character?	
Wanted... What did the character want?	
But... What was the problem?	
So... How did the character try to solve the problem?	
Then... How was the problem solved?	

Using the graphic organizer from above, write a summary of the book.

_____

_____

_____

_____

_____

_____

Figure 6.1. Somebody, Wanted, But

Researching Names

SL.1.4, SL.2.4, SL.3.4

Like many cultures in Bulgaria, people are given names that have a meaning. Ask students to research their names on the Internet or in a baby-naming book to find the meaning(s) and origin(s) and share with the class. Then tell students to imagine they lived in a culture where they had to give someone a new name against their will.

Next, have students create a PowerPoint slideshow informing the audience what that name would be and why. State its meaning and origin as well. Finally, have students use the narration tool for adding voice to their presentation.

Spotlight Bulgaria

SL.2.5, SL.3.5

Have students produce an episode on Bulgaria for the class weekly, bi-weekly, or monthly radio show. Student groups will create MP3 (Audacity) or MP4 (video) digital files to (1) report a glimpse of Bulgaria geography, history, and culture and (2) share the summary of a Bulgarian book(s) read.

HOLLAND
Boxes for Katje by Candace Fleming (2003)
Grade Levels: K–3
Themes: Caring, Friendship, Service, Seasons

Summary:

After the war, things were scarce in the tiny Dutch town of Olst. One day, Katje, a young Dutch girl, receives a package from an American friend, Rosie. Katje writes a thank-you letter back, and the communication of these girls continues as more packages are sent and Katje shares the gifts with the people in her town. Based on true events, Fleming's story teaches the importance of sharing and caring for others.

Country Information:

Holland is a province of the Kingdom of the Netherlands. Individuals who are from the Netherlands are called the "Dutch." It is a common misconception to refer only to the people who reside in Holland as Dutch instead of all citizens of the Netherlands. However, "Dutch" also refers to the official language and an ethnicity. Those who are ethnically Dutch are descendants of the Germanic and Gallo-Celtic populations.

The Netherlands are geographically significant due to a large part of the country existing below sea level, making its dykes vital to the preservation of its population and territory. The Kingdom of the Netherlands is a constitutional monarchy with King William Alexander serving as the chief of state.

Education is mandatory for the first ten years, and the literacy rate is very high at 99 percent. Dutch industries include agro-industries, electrical equipment, and electronics. Agricultural products include the Dutch cheese, Gouda, flower bulbs, cut flowers, vegetables, fruits, and potatoes.

LITERACY ACTIVITIES

Book Box

RL.K.I, RL.I.I, RL.2.I, RL.3.I

Show students the cover of the book. Tell students that this story takes place in Olst, Holland. Then point out the location of Holland using Google Earth or an app, map, or globe. Next, use the book box activity to stimulate students' thinking about the book *Boxes for Katje*.

In this activity, the teacher places several objects that are related to the story in a box prior to sharing the book with students. As the objects are shown, students are asked to make predictions about the story. Once all objects have been shown, the teacher asks students to make their final decision. Possible objects to include in the box are letters, an American flag, a picture of tulips and a mailman, chocolate, a pair of wool socks, a small box, sugar, soap, etc.

Story Mapping

RL.K.5, RL.I.5, RL.2.5, RL.3.5

Have students listen to or read the story *Boxes for Katje*. Then work as a whole class to discuss/review the major elements of the story. Next, have students fill in the story map (see figure 6.2) by dictating or writing what happened in that part of the story.

For example, beginning (who is the story about, where does the story place?), middle (when does it happen, what happens because of this action?), and end (how is the problem solved, how does the story end?) Finally, have each student share his/her story map with a partner.

Max B

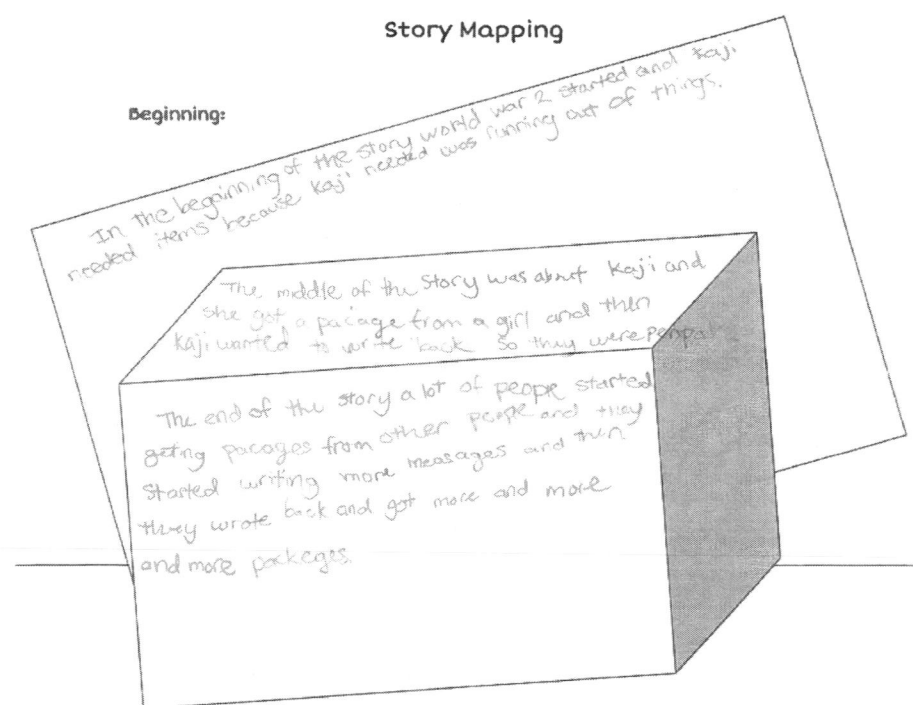

Story Mapping

Beginning:

In the beginning of the story world war 2 started and kaji needed items because kaji' needed was running out of things.

The middle of the story was about Kaji and she got a pacage from a girl and then Kaji wanted to write back so they were penpals

The end of the story a lot of people started geting pacages from other people and they started writing more measages and then they wrote back and got more and more and more packages.

Figure 6.2.   Story Mapping

Antonyms

L.2.5, L.3.5

Tell students that antonyms are words that have opposite meanings. List several examples on chart paper or a SmartBoard such as hot-cold, big-small, day-night, etc. Figure 6.3 presents an additional set of matching antonyms that teachers can share with students. In addition, the app Apples and Pairs can be used for practicing antonyms.

Next, have students work in pairs to complete Matching Antonyms in *Boxes for Katje* (appendix A) as they revisit the story to identify and write the antonym of the given word. Students will find the opposite of old, open, push, send, dark, etc. (the teacher may add other words to this list).

Mox B

Old	new
Open	close
Push	pull
Send	recive
Dark	bright

Activity 3: BOXES for KATJE

Figure 6.3.   Antonyms

Letter or Message Writing

RL.K.1, RL.1.1, RL.2.1, RL.3.1, SL.K.1, SL.1.1, SL.2.1, SL.3.1, W.K.7, W.1.7, W.2.7, W.3.7

In the story, Dutch families had many needs after World War II. Discuss with the students how meeting basic needs is sometimes difficult. Explain what are considered the basic needs of humans. Then find out about the local charitable organizations in your area and conduct a food/clothing drive to help meet the needs of families.

Next, have students work in small groups to design posters to place around the school. As the food/clothing is donated, have each group box the items and include a letter and message with it. Students will use the writing template (appendix A) for composing letters and digital devices for recording their messages.

Spotlight Holland

SL.2.5, SL.3.5

Have students produce an episode on Holland for the class weekly, bi-weekly, or monthly radio show. Student groups will create MP3 (Audacity) or MP4 (video) digital files to (1) report a glimpse of Holland geography, history, and culture and (2) share the summary of book(s) read from Holland.

ITALY
In English, Of Course by Josephine Nobisso (2002)
Grade Levels: K–3
Themes: Immigration, ELL, Linguistic Understanding

Summary:

Josephine, an immigrant from Italy, tries to express herself in English as her teacher helps find the words that she wants to describe. Nobisso's story, based on her true experience, will touch the hearts of the readers who are learning how to express themselves using a language that is not their native tongue.

Country Information:

The country of Italy is known for its cuisine, artistic culture, religious history, and legacy of an empire. The country includes several small islands and has two smaller sovereign states within its boundaries: Vatican City and the Republic of San Marino.

The majority of Italians practice Catholicism, a reflection of the country's strong historic ties to the church. The official language is Italian. Education is mandatory for twelve years, and 98 percent of the population is literate. The Italian government is a republic with an elected president and an appointed prime minister. The country joined the European Union in 1957 and adopted the Euro as its currency in 2002.

Italy has made many cultural contributions to the Western world. Most notably is its role in developing the Renaissance Age and producing artists such as Michelangelo and scientists like Galileo. Italian food is defined by its wine, pasta, seafood, oil, and cheeses. Italian agriculture produces grapes, olives, and beef, while its industries are mainly tourism, textiles, clothing, and machinery.

LITERACY ACTIVITIES

Anticipation Guides

RL.K.1, RL.1.1, RL.2.1, RL.3.1, SL.K.1, SL.1.1, SL.2.1, SL.3.1, W.K.7, W.1.7, W.2.7, W.3.7

Show students the cover of the book. Tell students that this story is about Josephine, an immigrant girl from Naples, Italy. Then point out the location of Italy using Google Earth, a map, or a globe. Ask students if they know anyone who has experienced linguistic misunderstandings. Allow time for students to share their responses.

Max B

Anticipation Guides for *In English of Course*

Before Reading		Statements	After Reading	
Agree	Disagree		Agree	Disagree
_____	√ _____	1. A new language is always easy to understand.	_____	√ _____
_____	√ _____	2. A new language is always easy to speak.	_____	√ _____
√ _____	_____	3. Being different is fun!	√ _____	_____
√ _____	_____	4. It's important to learn other languages.	√ _____	_____
√ _____	_____	5. The teacher provided Josephine with a good choice of words when helping her tell her story.	√ _____	_____

Figure 6.4.   Anticipation Guide

Then have students engage in an anticipation guide (Readance, Bean, and Baldwin 1989) to activate their prior knowledge and stimulate interest in the topic by responding to the five statements as shown in figure 6.4. To enhance the linguistic understanding of all students, have students work in pairs as they decide whether they agree or disagree with them.

Next, have students meet in small groups to share the reasons for their responses. After listening to or reading the selection, have students rethink their responses and make additional notes.

Sketch-to-Stretch

W.K.I

On the first day of school, Josephine experienced linguistic misunderstandings. Use the sketch-to-stretch (Harste, Short, and Burke 1988) strategy in the classroom to enable students to express their thoughts about what they read. It will also help students explore the text and expand their understanding.

First, model ways symbols can be used to illustrate linguistic understanding. Have students listen to or read a selection. Then allow students to express their thoughts through art by using lines, shapes, colors, pictures, and images. Finally, have students share their illustrations and explain what they mean.

Character Traits

RL.1.3, RL.2.3, RL.3.3

Character traits tell how a character acts or behaves in the story. Tell students that after they have heard or read the story, they will be given a literary report card (Johnson and Louis 1987). In this activity, they will analyze a character's traits. For example, when Josephine participated in the class activity, she knew she was in trouble because she knew little English. Therefore, she could be given a grade of "A" for being *brave*.

Tell students they will grade Josephine in three areas. They will give her a "G" for good, "S" for satisfactory, and "N" for needs to improve. In addition to assigning grades, students provide a reason for each grade in the comment section. See appendix A for a blank sample of the literary report card.

A Day in the Life of Josephine

RL.1.3, RL.2.3, RL.3.3, W.1.7, W.2.7, W.3.7

Ask students to pretend they are the character Josephine and had recently enrolled in a new school in a country where the language is different from their own. Have students talk about what it would be like. Then have students work in pairs and write a story about a day in the life of Josephine. Finally, students will create a digital story.

The storyteller combines narrative with digital content and video for making a three- to five-minute movie for their new television show called "A Day in the Life of Josephine." Be sure to focus on the 5 Ws and H. *Tell who is the main character, what happened, where it happened, when it happened, why it happened, and how it happened.*

Spotlight Italy

SL.2.5, SL.3.5

Have students produce an episode on Italy for the class weekly, bi-weekly, or monthly radio show. Student groups will create MP3 (Audacity) or MP4 (video) digital files to (1) report a glimpse of Italy geography, history, and culture and (2) share the summary of book(s) read from Italy.

TURKEY
The Hungry Coat: A Tale from Turkey by Demi (2004)
Grade Levels: K–3
Themes: True Friendship, Helping Others

Summary:

Nasrettin Hoca is a funny little wise man who wears a huge, white turban and a worn-out coat with many patches, and likes to help others. One day, he visits his friends for a banquet after helping people catch a loose goat. To his surprise, Nasrettin faces isolation from everyone and does not even get any food served, simply because of how he looks and smells.

When he returns washed and with his best coat, he surprises his friends by feeding his coat, saying that it was his coat that was invited to eat since when he was wearing his old coat, nobody wanted him to be there.

Through Nasrettin, Demi teaches the readers about how important it is to see a person from the inside and not to judge from the surface. Her beautiful artwork exposes the readers to traditional Turkish paintings as she brings to life Turkey's famous folk hero in the story.

Country Information:

The Republic of Turkey is the modern political descendant of the Ottoman Empire. Though the territory was greatly reduced, Turkey is still in control of a land mass a little bit larger than Texas. Turkey is also unfortunately situated in an area known for its frequent earthquakes. The country has much geographic importance with its control of the Turkish straits, which give access to the Black and Aegean seas.

Turkey is home to Turkish and Kurdish populations. Almost the entire country is Islamic, but small populations practice Christianity, Judaism, and Bahai. Turkish is the official language, though Kurdish, Armenian, and Greek can be heard. Education is mandatory for Turkish children for their first eight years. Unfortunately, there is a large divide between education for males and females, with an almost 20 percent difference between their literacy rates.

LITERACY ACTIVITIES

Learning About Turkey

RL.K.1, RL.1.1, RL.2.1, RL.3.1

Ask the students what they know about Turkey. Record their responses on chart paper. Use the Internet or an app, a map, Google Earth, or a globe to locate Turkey. Discuss with students how the story they are about to read is a folktale from Turkey.

Review the characteristics of a folktale, an old story passed down through the ages, usually embellishing on real or fictitious events and characters, usually containing a moral or teaching in the story. Take a picture walk and have students make predictions about the story. Share predictions.

Parts of a Story (Ball Toss)

RL.K.1, RL.1.1, RL.2.1, RL.3.1, SL.K.1, SL.1.1, SL.2.1, SL.3.1

Using an inflatable beach ball, cut out the questions (appendix A) and tape them onto the beach ball. In groups of five to six, have students toss the ball to one another and answer the question that their hand lands on to review the parts of the story.

Character Analysis

RL.K.3, RL.1.3, RL.2.3, RL.3.3

As a class, create a character web (Bromley 1996) with Nasrettin Hoca as the character. Begin by writing his name in the middle of the web. Tell students to assist you in identifying traits of Nasrettin. Next, for each trait that is chosen, ask students to assist you in providing evidence of the character's actions, words, and attitude.

Writing Folktales

SL.2.5, SL.3.5, W.2.3, W.3.3

Students will write their own folktales either individually or with a partner. Students can use pictures from clipart to support their text and read their book aloud using GarageBand or other digital recording devices.

Spotlight Turkey

SL.2.5, SL.3.5

Have students produce an episode on Turkey for the class weekly, bi-weekly, or monthly radio show. Student groups will create MP3 (Audacity) or MP4 (video) digital files to (1) report a glimpse of Turkey's geography, history, and culture and (2) share the summary of a Turkish book(s) read.

RELATED APPS AND WEB RESOURCES

Apps for Europe

- *GeoFlight Europe:* A fun interactive geography app offering a challenging learning environment. A simple game where your kids need to fly a little to various destinations on the European map.
- *Kids Maps—Europe:* Make geography fun for kids with an educational map puzzle game of Europe!
- *SlideShark!:* The folks at Brainshark have developed this app to be the missing link solution for showing PowerPoint on mobile devices—with the least amount of tinkering and headaches.
- *Let's Predict:* Select the cards you want students to see and have them use the cues in the pictures to figure out what happens next. You may also use these pictures to encourage conversational speech or as writing prompts.
- *The Story Map:* The Story Map is a free set of graphic organizers designed to help teachers and students in prewriting and postreading activities.

WEBSITES

Bulgaria

For Teachers:

Bulgaria

http://countries.mrdonn.org/easterneurope.html
Resources for lessons about Bulgaria.

Bulgarian Eggs

http://www.papereggs.com/pysanky.htm
Tons of templates to color Bulgarian eggs.

For Students:

Kid World
Citizen
Bulgaria

http://kidworldcitizen.org/category/europe/bulgaria/
Activities for kids about Bulgarian culture.

Holland

For Teachers:

Holland

http://countries.mrdonn.org/benelux.html
Resources for lessons about Holland.

Netherland
Activities

http://www.dltk-kids.com/world/netherlands/
In-class activities about Netherlands culture.

For Students:

Cyberkids-
Holland

http://www.cyberkidzgames.com/cyberkidz/game.php?spelUrl=
library/creatief/groep1/creatief5/&spelNaam=Dutch%20road%
20signs&groep=1&vak=creatief
Games about Holland road signs.

Turkey

For Teachers:

Turkey Flag

http://www.proteacher.com/redirect.php?goto=5163
Printable version of the Turkey flag to color.

Turkey
Resources

http://countries.mrdonn.org/turkey.html
Resources for lessons on Turkey.

For Students:

http://kids.nationalgeographic.com/kids/places/find/turkey/
Photos, facts, and videos on Turkey.

*National
Geographic
Turkey*

http://www.smm.org/catal/
Interactive game about an archaeological dig in Turkey.

*Interactive
Game Turkey*

7

CENTRAL AMERICA

BELIZE
Jahmon's Adventure Home by Bill W. Hash (2014)
Grade Levels: 2–3
Themes: Kindness

Summary:

    Jahmon's Adventure Home is an imaginative tale about a boy lost from home. The story focuses on the value of selflessness and working as a group. The author uses traditional Creole (complete with interpretations) in order to distinguish between narration and Jahmon's family speech. The illustrations are friendly and fun.

Country Information:

    Located in Central America, Belize is one of the regions where former Mayan cities can be found. Today, direct Mayan descendants can still be found around the country. The majority of Belizeans are mestizo, meaning a mix between native peoples and the Spanish. English is the official language but Creole, Spanish, and Mayan are spoken by significant portions of the population.

    Belize shares a border with Guatemala, and disagreements about territorial boundaries have been the source of tension between the two countries. What is unique about Belize is its population disbursement; only half the population lives in urban centers with the other half spread out in the countryside.

    Also remarkable for Belize is that the median age of its residents is twenty and much of its population is under the age of fourteen. The Belizean government is a parliamentary democracy, with Queen Elizabeth II serving as head of state. A governor representing the queen in the country is advised by the prime minister and cabinet.

LITERACY ACTIVITIES

Directed Reading-Thinking Activity (DR-TA)

RL.K.1, RL.1.1, RL.2.1, RL.3.1

Show students the cover of the book. Tell students that this story takes place in Belize. Then point out the location of Belize using the Internet, an app, a map, Google Earth, or a globe. Next, use the strategy DR-TA (Stauffer 1980) to engage students in making predictions to assist them in reading for a purpose. Have at least two to five predetermined stopping points.

Ask students to read or listen to the selection title. Ask students what they think will happen in the story and why they think that. Record the students' responses on chart paper or a SmartBoard. Then students read or listen to the first selection. Then stop to confirm or reject their predictions. The teacher may ask questions such as (1) What do you think will happen next? (2) What do you think would happen if . . . ? (3) Why do you think so? (4) What prediction did you make?, and (5) What information in the story made you think that?

Students continue to repeat this process until the end of the story.

Alphabetical Order

L.1.6, L.2.6, L.3.6

List character names on chart paper as students recall them. Characters include: Jahmon, Grandfather, Alberto, Gilbert, Raymundo, Omar, Maria, and Leoni. Students work with partners to illustrate and label an assigned character from the generated list. Students holding their character drawing come to the front of the room and try to put characters in alphabetical order.

Could It Be True?

RL.K.9, RL.1.9, RL.3.9

In Jahmon's adventure there is a blend of realistic and fantasy events (see figure 7.1). Review the story with students. List events in sequential order on chart paper as students recall them. Students will work in small groups to illustrate an assigned event on paper from the generated list.

Next, create two columns titled REALISTIC and FANTASY on chart paper or a SmartBoard. Collect the illustrations. Hold up an illustration, have students explain the event, and categorize it as reality or fantasy. Continue with the remaining illustrations. Events will include:

- Jahmon's grandfather carving a dory
- Jahmon going fishing with his grandfather
- a storm coming
- the dory capsizing
- Jahmon getting carried away by a sea turtle
- Jahmon meeting and talking to animals
- animals helping Jahmon get home

Could it be True?

While discussing whether illustrations from the story are realistic or fantasy, record your thoughts below in the appropriate column. Compare your chart to the class chart and discuss findings.

Realistic   **Fantasy**

Figure 7.1.   Could It Be True?

Letter Writing

RL.K.6, RL.1.6, RL.2.6, RL.3.6, W.K.3, W.1.3, W.2.3, W.3.3

Brainstorm with students the purpose of writing a letter. Bring in examples of various types of letters including thank-you notes, invitations, postcards, etc.

After reviewing parts of a letter, students pretend they are Jahmon and write a letter to Alberto and his friends thanking them for saving him. Have students include events such as what happened when he returned home. Help each child record his/her letter using any digital recording device. Students will listen to recorded letters and identify various greetings, main body ideas, and closings used by their peers.

Spotlight Belize

SL.2.5, SL.3.5

Have students produce an episode on Belize for the class weekly, bi-weekly, or monthly radio show. Student groups will create MP3 (Audacity) or MP4 (video) digital files to (1) report a glimpse of Belize's geography, history, and culture and (2) share the summary of a Belizian book(s) read.

COSTA RICA
The Remembering Stone **by Barbara Timberlake Russell (2004)**
Grade Levels: K–3
Themes: Family, Dreams

Summary:
Barbara Timberlake Russell's book features a young girl named Ana and her mother. Ana's mother is from Costa Rica, and her dream to return to her home inspires Ana to build her own dream. The different adults that Ana speaks to about dreams paint a soft picture of how humans incorporate hope into their lives. Spanish words and phrases are used creatively throughout the book.

Country Information:
The Republic of Costa Rica is a warm tropical island with lush forests. Costa Rica is known for its incredible biodiversity and is home to more bird life than is seen in the entire North American continent (approximately 850 different species). Despite its small size (comparable to West Virginia), Costa Rica is also home to two active volcanoes and two inactive volcanoes. One of Costa Rica's natural resources is hydroelectric power.

The majority of Costa Ricans are of Spanish descent with a recently emerging mestizo population. Roman Catholicism is the dominant religion of the country, with Protestant religions being represented in much smaller populations. Spanish is the official language, but some areas have a Creole language with English influences. The majority of the working population in Costa Rica is service based, but there is a significant agricultural workforce. Many agricultural products, such as bananas and pineapples, are exported to the United States.

LITERACY ACTIVITIES

Book Box

RL.K.1, RL.1.1, RL.2.1, RL.3.1

Show students the cover of the book. Tell students that this story takes place in Costa Rica. Then point out the location of Costa Rica using the Internet, an app, a map, Google Earth, or a globe. Before reading the story to students reveal items from the book box. Items may include:

- a stuffed bird
- slice of bread or bread crumbs in a bag
- a necklace with a locket
- a black stone with yellow and red flecks painted on
- picture of a volcano
- a notebook

Let students know that each item plays a part in the story. Have students make predictions as to what they will be reading about using items from the book box and prior knowledge.

Guess the Word

RF.2.4, RF.3.4

Take sentences from the story and write them on chart paper or a Smart-Board. Then cover one word with sticky note. Read the sentences to the class. Have students try to recall what happened in the story and guess the covered word. If students struggle while figuring out the word, uncover the first letter to give them the first sound.

My Favorite Locket

L.2.1, L.3.1

Students will design a locket using construction paper. Inside the locket on the left-hand side, students will illustrate and write a sentence about their favorite event from the story. On the right-hand side, students will recall and write the title, author, characters, and setting of the story. Once students have completed this task, they will make the locket into a necklace using yarn. Students will wear and share their lockets with the class.

Dreams

W.K.3, W.1.3, W.2.3, W.3.3, W.K.6, W.1.6, W.2.6, W.3.6

Brainstorm with students their dreams and list on chart paper or a SmartBoard. Students will write a narrative about a dream they wish to accomplish. Working with the students, create a class digital story using images that pertain to their dreams. Combine narrative with digital content and video for making a three- to five-minute movie. Share the story with other classes or at a parent event.

Spotlight Costa Rica

SL.2.5, SL.3.5

Have students produce an episode on Costa Rica for the class weekly, bi-weekly, or monthly radio show. Student groups will create MP3 (Audacity) or MP4 (video) digital files to (1) report a glimpse of Costa Rica's geography, history, and culture and (2) share the summary of a Costa Rican book(s) read.

EL SALVADOR
***Alfredito Flies Home* by Jorge Arugueta (2007)**
Grades: K–3
Themes: Family, Moving, Refugees

Summary:

The story of Alfredito and his family reflects the story of many other El Salvadorian families who fled war-torn El Salvador for other places. Alfredito's recollection of the terrifying trip to America parallels his nervousness and excitement about returning to his original home to visit family.

Other characters from El Salvador represent the tragedy of split families. However, once Alfredito and his family land in El Salvador they are greeted with warmth and love. *Alfredito Flies Home* is an excellent book about what makes a family and a home.

Country Information:

In Central America the Republic of El Salvador is the smallest country but has one of the fastest-growing economies. El Salvador earns this distinction despite recovering from a recent civil war and various natural disasters such as hurricanes and the eruption of one of its volcanoes in 2005.

Many people coming into the country come for its beautiful mountains and beaches, while others are visiting home, like Alfredito. El Salvador is primarily an agricultural-producing country but has an emerging industrial sector. Almost half of the country's population lives in the capital city, San Salvador.

Many El Salvadorians struggle with obtaining access to basic necessities, and over 30 percent of the population lives below the poverty line. Literacy rates are also much lower than seen in the United States, with only nine years of mandatory education.

The political climate in El Salvador is tense. The country is a republic and has a multiparty system. In fact, San Salvador's mayor is from the communist political party FMLN (Farabundo Marti National Liberation Front) and the president is from ARENA (Nationalist Republican Alliance Party), a democratic party.

These two parties are the most powerful in politics and are reformed coalitions from the civil war. The economy in El Salvador is heavily influenced by the United States. For example, their currency is the dollar and they do not mint their own money.

LITERACY ACTIVITIES

Place to Place

RL.K.1, RL.1.1, RL.2.1, RL.3.1, RL.K.3, RL.1.3, RL.2.3, RL.3.3

Activate students' prior knowledge by asking, "Have you ever moved to a different place and how did it make you feel?" Brainstorm with students the reasons for moving to a different place. Tell students that the character, Alfredito, moved to another country with his parents. Students will make inferences and predictions as the story is read.

Compare and Contrast

RI.K.3, RI.1.3, RI.2.3, RI.3.3, RL.K.9, RL.1.9, RL.2.9, RL.3.9

Provide students with a copy of a Venn diagram (appendix A). Have them compare and contrast the cultures of the United States and El Salvador. Students find information in the book, online, or use apps for Central America. Some ideas might include:

- games and parties, piñatas versus pin the tail on the donkey
- Christmas traditions

Language Boxes

L.K.2, L.1.2, L.2.2, L.3.2, L.K.4, L.1.4, L.2.4, L.3.4

Using the words in the book glossary, students will create language boxes by folding paper into eight sections. In each box students will write the Spanish and English version of the word using the app Free Translator and illustrate it. Once students complete this project the class will echo read the words to reinforce the pronunciation and meaning.

Research

W.1.7, W.2.7, W.3.7, W.1.8, W.2.8, W.3.8

Using the Internet, students work with a partner to research another country from a teacher-generated list. Provide students with a copy of Special Celebrations (figure 7.2) and record their findings using a digital device. Allow time for students to share in class.

Spotlight El Salvador

SL.2.5, SL.3.5

Have students produce an episode on El Salvador for the class weekly, bi-weekly, or monthly radio show. Student groups will create MP3 (Audacity) or MP4 (video) digital files to (1) report a glimpse of El Salvador's geography, history, and culture and (2) share the summary of book(s) from El Salvador.

RELATED APPS AND WEB RESOURCES

Apps for Central America

- *iWorldGeography Central America:* Geography information for countries located in Central America.
- *elsalvador:* News and information about El Salvador.
- *TapQuiz World Edition:* Quiz yourself and others on country geography.
- *Kids Maps Apps:* Making geography fun!

Special Celebrations!

1. What is one holiday/celebration your country celebrates?

_____

_____

2. What are some special traditions that are related to this holiday/celebration?

_____

_____

_____

_____

_____

_____

3. Do we have a holiday/celebration that is similar? If yes, please explain.

_____

_____

_____

_____

_____

Figure 7.2.   Special Celebrations

WEBSITES

Belize

For Teachers:

National
Geographic
Belize

http://www.nationalgeographic.com/features/00/earthpulse/class
room.html#elementary
Belize videos and activities.

Macmillan
Belize Social
Studies

http://www.macmillan-caribbean.com/home/resources.aspx?Id=48
Lesson plans, videos, worksheets, answer sheets, sound files,
teacher's guides, and flash cards.

Teachers for a
Better Belize

http://www.tfabb.org/
Nonprofit website for teachers to learn about Belize and how
they can help.

For Students:

Kid World

http://kidworldcitizen.org/category/the-americas/belize/
A website with interesting information, photos, and videos
geared toward a young audience.

Facts About
Belize

http://ambergriscaye.com/pages/town/factsbze.html
General information students can easily use including climate,
population, geography, and history.

Costa Rica

For Teachers:

http://www.centralamerica.com/cr/index.htm
   A great, concise site with information on Costa Rican history, ecology, geography, and arts and culture.

Costa Rican History

http://www.proteacher.com/redirect.php?Goto=550
   These lesson plans were developed by a teacher in Illinois.

ROOM 16 Adventures in Costa Rica

For Students:

http://kids.nationalgeographic.com/kids/places/find/costa-rica/
   Photos, facts, and videos on Costa Rica.

National Geographic Costa Rica

El Salvador

For Teachers:

http://www.proteacher.com/redirect.php?goto=1772
   El Salvador flag outline for coloring.

El Salvador Flag

http://www.teachingforchange.org/wp-content/uploads/2012/08/askmeabout-storyenglish-wilfredo.pdf
   Story about a boy growing up in El Salvador.

Teaching for Change

*Justice and the
Generals*

http://www.pbs.org/wnet/justice/education/lp1.html

This site has a full lesson plan that extends five to six periods. It teaches about the country's social and political history and recommends additional resources and activities through websites.

Lesson Planet

http://www.lessonplanet.com/lesson-plans/el-salvador

Calls itself a "search engine for teachers." Offers various lesson plans, worksheets, and presentations, sorts according to grades, and has ratings.

For Students:

*National
Geographic El
Salvador*

http://kids.nationalgeographic.com/kids/places/find/el-salvador/

Photos, facts, and videos on El Salvador.

*Ducksters—
Brief History of
El Salvador*

http://www.ducksters.com/geography/country.php?Country=El%20Salvador

Kid-friendly website for general information about El Salvador.

*Countries and
Their Cultures:
El Salvador*

http://www.everyculture.com/Cr-Ga/El-Salvador.html

Cultural information on El Salvador with pictures.

8

NORTH AMERICA

AFRICAN AMERICAN
A Sweet Smell of Roses **by Angela Johnson (2005)**
Grade Levels: K–3
Themes: Diversity, Race, Civil Rights Movement, Martin Luther King Jr.

Summary:

Two children sneak out of the house to join the freedom march, playing a role in the civil rights movement. The smell of roses is mentioned throughout the story as they start to feel the sweetness of freedom. Velasquez's simple use of charcoal and the red for the American flag, teddy bear's ribbon, and roses leaves a strong impact to the "march to freedom."

Historical Information:

In American history, the 1950s through the 1960s were defined by the formation of peoples and organizations seeking empowerment and equality in all sectors of society. Foremost of these organizations was the National Association for the Advancement of Colored People (NAACP), with activist individuals, such as Martin Luther King Jr., leading marches and rallies. It was not uncommon for these groups to be met with open hostility, violence, and extreme prejudice.

An important turning point in the civil rights movement was a televised march in Birmingham, Alabama. In May 1963, Martin Luther King Jr. and other local activists organized a series of protests and marches decrying racist policies inherent in commerce and political procedures. On May 3 a march, which included several children, was underway when the local police turned fire hoses and dogs on the marchers. Footage and pictures taken of the event shocked the nation and motivated more of the American population to pressure the government for change. The following year the Civil Rights Act of 1964, guaranteeing equal rights to all citizens, was passed.

LITERACY ACTIVITIES

Text to World Connections

RL.K.9, RL.1.9, RL.2.9, RL.3.9

Ask the students if they have ever visited a historic site. Tell them that they will learn about a historic site in Birmingham, Alabama. Let students know that this is one of the places where people marched for freedom. Point out the location using Google Maps or other search engines. Tell students as they listen to or read, they will make text to world connections. Inform students that at one point in time in the United States, not all people were given the freedom of choice.

Next, select a category (for example, students wearing red) and tell them that they no longer have the right to have recess, but are to stay inside and clean the cafeteria. Ask the students if it is fair for those who lost their rights simply because they were wearing red. Connect the idea to how the African Americans did not have rights because of their skin color.

Marching for Rights

SL.1.1, SL.2.1, SL.3.1, W.1.1, 1.2.1, W.3.1

Why did the girls and other people march in the story? What does it mean to have rights and freedom? What would life be like without the rights written in the Constitution? Have the students discuss these topics and pretend to be a citizen in the past, convincing them how important it is for everyone, no matter what skin color or gender, to have their rights. Have students give their point of view and write the reasons they would march using the foot pattern I March Because (appendix A).

Four Square Vocabulary

L.K.4, L.1.4, L.2.4, L.3.4

Select three to five unfamiliar words to teach. Students will use a variety of strategies to assist in visualizing the meaning of words using the four square technique (Frayer, Frederick, and Klausmeier 1969; Stahl 2004). As shown in

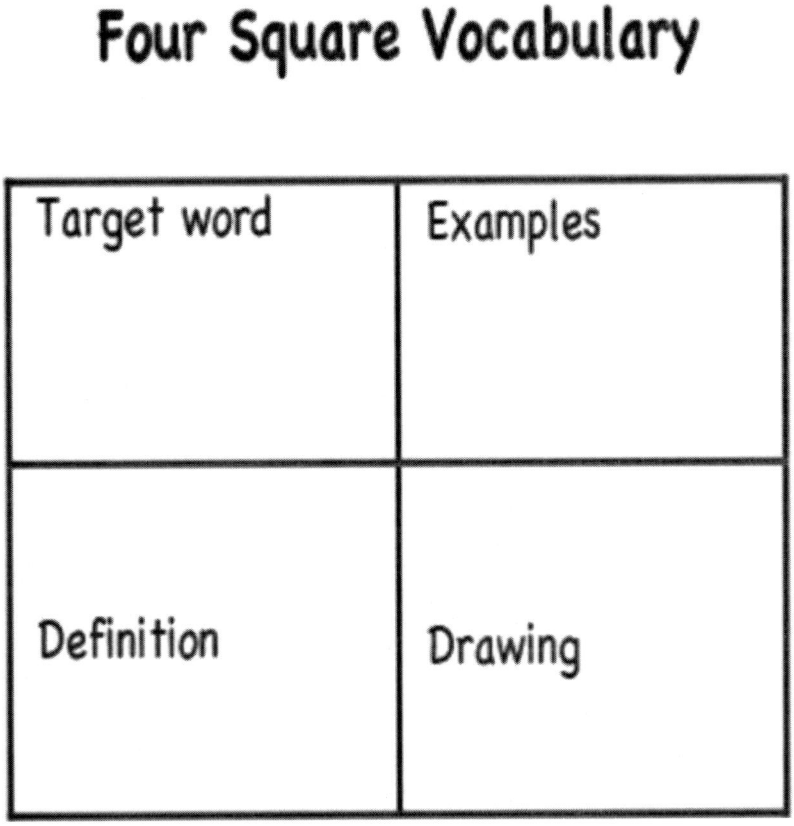

Four Square Vocabulary

Target word	Examples
Definition	Drawing

Figure 8.1.   Four Square Vocabulary

figure 8.1, have students write the target word in the upper left-hand corner. Then have students write what the word means in the lower left-hand corner. Next, have students provide examples of the word in the upper right-hand corner and write the word in a sentence in the lower right-hand corner.

I Have My Dream

RL.K.1, RL.1.1, RL.2.1, RL.3.1, W.K.1, W.1.1, W.2.1, W.3.1

Listen to Dr. Martin Luther King Jr.'s speech "I Have a Dream" (http://www.stanford.edu/group/King/). What are the things he wanted to see for children of the future? Have the students think about what they wish to see change for children of all cultures in the world right now. Then have students work in pairs or in a small group to write their own "I Have My Dream" speech. Next, have them create a class PowerPoint slideshow. Use narration to add voice to the presentation.

Spotlight Civil Rights

SL.2.5, SL.3.5

Have students produce an episode on civil rights for the class weekly, bi-weekly, or monthly radio show. In this episode, student groups will create segments using MP3 (Audacity) or MP4 (video) digital files to (1) report a glimpse of the purpose for the freedom marches and (2) share book(s) read about civil rights.

The Other Side **by Jacqueline Woodson (2001)**
Grade Levels: K–3
Themes: Segregation, Friendship, Difference, Acceptance

Summary:
There was a fence that stretched through a town and nobody climbed over to the other side. Clover, an African American girl, lived on one side, and Annie, a Caucasian girl, lived on the other. Annie always sat on the fence, and one day the two girls converse and start spending time together, and they hope that, one day, the fence will be taken down and there will be no sides. Lewis's beautiful illustrations portray children who see beyond their skin color to form a friendship.

Historic Information:
From the 1600s to 1865, the year slavery was abolished through the Emancipation Proclamation (though this is contested), slavery was integrated in American society, politics, and economics, especially in the heavily agricultural southern states.

The Civil War was just as much a political- and economic-based war as it was a moral one. While the abolitionist Harriet Beecher Stowe appealed to the hearts of the average American through her book *Uncle Tom's Cabin*, politicians and businessmen were attempting to justify America's dependence on the system.

Even after slavery was abolished, its legacy would continue until laws and reforms, such as the Civil Rights Act of 1964, guaranteed equal rights and protection for all American citizens. In later years, there was a push for equality in schools. In 1954 the Supreme Court decided in *Brown v. Board of Education* that schools should no longer be segregated.

LITERACY ACTIVITIES

Making Connections

SL.K.I, SL.I.I, SL.2.I, SL.3.I, RL.K.9, RL.I.9, RL.2.9, RL.3.9

Tell students that the story they are about to listen to or read is told from the point of view of Clover, the African American girl. It is about two girls who are separated by a fence. Ask students if they have ever been separated from someone against their will.

Split the classroom in half using something visible (for example, using string or putting desks in the middle to create boundaries) and have the students talk with the people on their side and the other side for few minutes. Put the class back together and discuss what it was like and how they felt. Then have the students reflect and share their experience of being separated or segregated from part of the class.

Ten Important Words

L.K.5, L.1.5, L.2.5, L.3.5, SL.K.1, SL.1.1, SL.2.1, SL.3.1

Students complete this activity during reading. Give each student ten Post-it notes. Ask students to write the ten most important words (Stephens and Brown 2000; Yopp and Yopp 2002) while they read. Once the students have completed this task, create a bar graph and look for patterns as students share their most important words. For example, which words are least/most selected, etc.

Discussion Web

RL.K.1, RL.1.1, RL.2.1, RL.3.1, SL.K.1, SL.1.1, SL.2.1, SL.3.1

Provide each student a copy of the Discussion Web (Alverman 1991), as shown in figure 8.2, to encourage active participation in this activity. First,

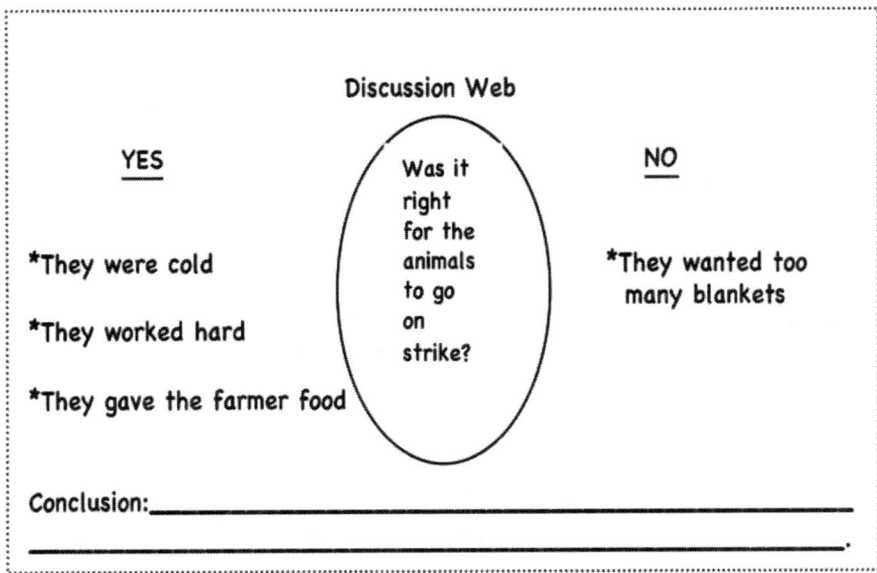

Figure 8.2.   Discussion Web

introduce the guiding question for completing the web. For example, *"Was it right for Clover and Annie to spend time together?"* Next, have students work in pairs, taking turns writing an equal amount of words or phrases in both the "yes" and "no" columns.

Before they have enough time to fill up the blanks, have two pairs form a new group of four to compare responses. Together, this group will come to consensus on "yes" or "no" responses. Then have students select a spokesperson from each group who will explain the group's point of view to the class.

Writing a Press Release

SL.K.1, SL.1.1, SL.2.1, SL.3.1, W.K.1, W.1.1, W.2.1, W.3.1

Have students work in pairs or small groups. Tell them to pretend they are the town reporter. Their job is to write a press release that will be submitted to the newspaper and television station in support of their argument for or against the fence that runs through town. Have students record their story using a digital recording device.

Spotlight Segregation

SL.2.5, SL.3.5

Have students produce an episode on the unfairness of segregation for the class weekly, bi-weekly, or monthly radio show. In this episode, student groups will create segments using MP3 (Audacity) or MP4 (video) digital files to (1) report a glimpse of hurtful acts of segregation and (2) share book(s) on social justice.

AMERICAN INDIAN, MUSCOGEE
Jingle Dancer by Cynthia Smith (2000)
Grades: K–3
Themes: Dance, Family, Tradition, Sharing, Respect

Summary:

Tink, tink, tink. Jenna, a member of the Muscogee Nation and also of Ojibway descent, wants to jingle dance like her grandma but doesn't have the jingles to sew on her dress. Jenna goes on a search for jingles and borrows from her relatives and friends who cannot perform in the powwow and is asked to dance for them. Van Wright and Hu's beautiful use of watercolor brings up Jenna's excitement to dance.

Historical Information:

The Muscogee, or "Creek," Indians were a collection of tribes located within what became the southeastern United States. The name Creek comes from the location of their town, primarily along rivers. Prior to the arrival of European settlers, the Creek Indians absorbed other tribes through warfare. After Europeans began a campaign that violently challenged tribal authority, the Creek began to absorb the displaced Indians.

In the early 1800s the U.S. government began to push tribes out of the southern states and into the west. Treaties were made guaranteeing the tribes' control over land in Oklahoma, but the Civil War made the new land anything but peaceful. Until the 1970s the Creek tribes were often challenged by the U.S. government in terms of land ownership and tribal independence through various policies. During the 1970s the tribes were given sovereignty over their own lands and could elect their own officials.

LITERACY ACTIVITIES

Learning Across Cultures

RL.K.1, RL.1.1, RL.2.1, RL.3.1, SL.K.1, SL.1.1, SL.2.1, SL.3.1

Tell students that this story is about a Muscogee girl who lives in a small town in Oklahoma. Use an app, a map, or Google Earth to locate Oklahoma. Next, ask the students to draw a picture of a Native American and/or write what they know about them. Discuss the Muscogee (Creek) Indians' culture. Tell students that Jenna wants to honor her family's tradition. Ask the students if they have any family traditions. List students' responses on chart paper or a SmartBoard.

Double Entry Journal

RL.K.1, RL.1.1, RL.2.1, RL.3.1, W.K.1, W.1.1, W.2.1, W.3.1

Tell students after hearing or reading the story that they will use a double-entry journal to respond to the readings. Give each student a sheet of the Double Entry Journal (appendix A). On the left side of the journal, they will copy quotes from the selection that are meaningful to them. On the right side, they will write their reaction to the quote.

For example, the teacher may write the following on a SmartBoard: "Again and again, Jenna watched a videotape of Grandma Wolfe jingle dancing." Then on the right side write, "This reminds me of the time my grandma sent us a video. She wasn't able to travel to our house for the holidays, so she sent us a message on video. We watched it again and again." Students can also respond to the readings by dictating or drawing a picture. Allow time for sharing responses.

Understanding Personification

RL.K.2, RL.1.2, RL.2.2, RL.3.2

Tell students that personification is when the author gives human traits such as feeling or action to nonliving things. In the story, the author uses personification to describe the times of day:

> Moon kissed Sun good night
> Sun caught a glimpse of Moon

Discuss the object being personified and what the author is saying by using personification. Then have students work in pairs or in small group to identify additional personifications in the story and write the meaning of the personification. Finally, have students write their own original sentences.

Think Aloud

RL.1.10, RL.2.10, RL.3.10

Demonstrate the Think Aloud strategy (Davey 1983; Wilhelm 2001) to show students how to construct meaning from a selection before, during, and after reading. The teacher will stop periodically to think out loud about what he/she has read. Then have students read a selection at an appropriate level in pairs, small groups, or with the teacher as they practice using this strategy. As the students read, they will be asked to stop and reflect on what they have read.

Letter Writing

RL.K.1, RL.1.1, RL.2.1, RL.3.1

Students will write a letter to Jenna or Grandma Wolfe. They will ask questions about the tradition of jingle dancing. Have students read their letters several times. Once they are comfortable with it, have each student record their information using Audacity.

Spotlight Native Americans

SL.2.5, SL.3.5

Have students produce a Native American episode for the class weekly, bi-weekly, or monthly radio show. In this episode, student groups will create segments using MP3 (Audacity) or MP4 (video) digital files to (1) report a glimpse of the Muscogee, or "Creek," Indians' culture and (2) share book(s) on Native Americans.

MUSCOGEE INDIANS
The Good Luck Cat **by Joy Harjo (2000)**
Grade Levels: K–3
Themes: Native Americans, Good Luck

Summary:

A Native American girl believes that her cat Woogie is a good luck cat because it has gone through many lives. When Woogie disappears from her, the girl worries that her luck may have run out and may not return again. Lee captures the expressions and movements of the cat throughout the story.

LITERACY ACTIVITIES

Activating Prior Knowledge

RI.1.10, RI.2.10, RI.3.10

Show students the cover of the book and have them predict what the story might be about. Then tell students that the story they are about to listen to or read is about a girl who has a cat. Have students share what they know about cats. Record their responses on chart paper or a SmartBoard. Then tell students that the unnamed girl who narrates the story feels she has a good luck cat. Discuss with the students about what brings luck to them. Do they wear or carry something on special days when they want luck?

Enhancing Vocabulary

L.K.4, L.1.4, L.2.4, L.3.4

Explain the concept of base word and suffix. Check for understanding. Preselect a list of action words and have students work in pairs to identify base words and the suffix "-ed." Then provide students access to the app Puppy Pop which is a fun way to build their understanding of suffixes. Next, have students go on a word search for actions words (-ed) in the story. Ask students to read the words and record them in their vocabulary notebook.

Feelings Chart

SL.K.1, SL.1.1, SL.2.1, SL.3.1, W.K.1, W.1.1, W.2.1, W.3.1, RL.K.1, RL.1.1, RL.2.1, RL.3.1

As a whole group, list the events of the story and discuss the girl's feelings for each of the events. Then individually, have the students think about a time when they lost something (for example, pets, objects). Have students write out the events on the left-hand side of the chart. Then on the right-hand side of the chart have students write their feelings/reaction to the events. See appendix A for a blank sample.

Point of View

RL.K.6, RL.1.6, RL.2.6, RL.3.6

Have the students rewrite the story from the cat's point of view using the Point of View Template (figure 8.3). Ask students what the cat felt each time he was about to lose his life. For example, when he ran in front of a car or was spinning and yowling in the dryer or in the trunk of the car, etc. Be creative. After completing the Point of View activity, have students record their stories using a digital recording device.

Figure 8.3. Point of View Template

Spotlight Muscogee Indians

SL.2.5, SL.3.5

Have students produce a Native American episode for the class weekly, bi-weekly, or monthly radio show. In this episode, student groups will create segments using MP3 (Audacity) or MP4 (video) digital files to (1) report a glimpse of the Muscogee, or "Creek," Indians' history and (2) make connections to other books about Muscogee Indians.

INTERRACIAL AMERICANS
Family **by Isabell Monk (2001)**
Grade Levels: K–3
Themes: Family, Biracial, Cooking, Love

Summary:

Hope, the child of a Caucasian father and an African American mother, visits her aunt on her mother's side for a family reunion. Every person brings a family dish to share, each uniquely made. Hope also brings her unique dish that she learned from her father's side and adds to the family sharing. Porter's colorful illustration portrays a happy multiracial family who shares and celebrates with family love.

Historical Information:

In the late eighteenth century Thomas Jefferson made the suggestion that American colonists and Native Americans should be encouraged to marry and merge their cultures together. Two hundred years later, a Virginian judge residing over a case of interracial marriage made the statement that the different races were on separate continents for a reason. As late as the 1960s some states in the United States made it an illegal act for people of different races to marry each other. However, in 1967, the case of Loving v. Virginia made it illegal to enforce such laws in the United States.

The number of people born of biracial unions is growing at a rapid rate. Today, as teachers work to develop a more culturally sensitive classroom to reflect the diverse student population, they must include not only children's literature on Asian, Native American, African, and Mexican children but also sufficient interracial children's literature. It is extremely important for interracial students to be exposed to informational and narrative texts that represent family settings and life experiences like their own.

LITERACY ACTIVITIES

My Family

RL.K.1, RL.1.1, RL.2.1, RL.3.1, SL.K.1, SL.1.1, SL.2.1, SL.3.1, W.K.3, W.1.3, W.2.3, W.3.3

Show students the cover of the book. Students use their imagination as they make story predictions. Tell students that the story they are about to listen to or read is about family and every family is unique.

Ask students to think about and describe their families by drawing and/or writing. After discussing what a family is, have the students draw their homes and describe anything unique about them. Have the students draw a picture of their family at home. Allow time for students to share.

Writing an Invitation

SL.K.1, SL.1.1, SL.2.1, SL.3.1, W.K.2, W.1.2, W.2.2, W.3.2

Discuss with the students about a family gathering. Ask students to share different types of occasions for family gatherings. List students' response on chart paper or a SmartBoard. Next, have the students write an invitation to a family gathering that they are going to host. Brainstorm ideas about what to include in the invitation (for example, occasion, place, date, time, what to bring, etc.). See appendix A for a blank sample.

Practicing Phrasing

RF.K.4, RF.1.4, RF.2.4, RF.3.4

Tell students that they will reread the story in pairs or in small groups in a variety of ways. Begin by showing students how to use correct phrasing. Write a sentence or two on chart paper or the SmartBoard and read it aloud once or twice. Then reread the sentences again, having students echo each sentence as it is read.

Next, have students read chorally as phrases are identified. Stop and check students' understanding of phrasing. Finally, have students reread the story as they practice phrasing in pairs or small groups.

Making a Recipe Book

SL.K.1, SL.1.1, SL.2.1, SL.3.1, W.K.2, W.1.2, W.2.2, W.3.2

Discuss the different kinds of food the students eat at home. Are there dishes they cook for special occasions? Have the students ask about a recipe made at home which they would like to share with classmates. Discuss the recipes (what is in a recipe?) and create an electronic class recipe book using PowerPoint. Have students add narration to the presentation.

Spotlight Families

SL.2.5, SL.3.5

Have students produce an Interracial American episode for the class weekly, bi-weekly, or monthly radio show. In this episode, student groups will create segments using MP3 (Audacity) or MP4 (video) digital files to (1) report a glimpse of the uniqueness of different families and (2) share.

Am I a Color Too? by Heidi Cole and Nancy Vogl (2005)
Grade Levels: K–3
Themes: Family, Ethnicity

Summary:
In this poem, Tyler has a father whom everyone calls black and a mother whom everyone calls white, and he wonders if he is a color too. He sees people dream, feel, and love in every color and he decides that it doesn't matter what color he is because he is just like everyone else. Purnell's insightful illustrations of people of different races portray that the skin color does not tells us who we are.

Historical Information:
After segregation came to an end, people still worked to keep mixed relationships from occurring. While schools were compelled by law to desegregate, social events like high school proms remained open to community pressure. In 2002 Gerica McCrary, a high school student, protested her school's encouragement of the student body maintaining two separate proms: one for white students and one for African Americans. However, as American society continues to confront and tackle racism, biracialism will cease to be exceptional and may instead better reflect Jefferson's wish.

LITERACY ACTIVITIES

I Wonder

RL.K.I. RL.I.I, RL.2.I, RL.3.I

Ask students if they know what it means to wonder about something. Then ask them if they have ever wondered about anything. Record their response on chart paper or a SmartBoard. Tell students to listen carefully or read the poem independently to find out about what things the boy wonders about.

Word Sort

L.K.4, L.I.4, L.2.4, L.3.4

Have students work in small groups and create their own word sort using words from the poem. Once all the words have been sorted, ask each group to switch sorts. Allow groups time to categorize the new word sorts. Have students switch sorts once more to engage and discern patterns of similarity among words. Finally, ask each group to read words aloud and describe the common features.

Five Senses Poem

W.K.2, W.I.2, W.2.2, W.3.2

Have students write a Five Senses Poem (see figure 8.4) about people using their five senses. Tell students that this poem contains five lines, one for each sense (see, hear, touch, taste, and smell). Students may add an extra line if they wish.

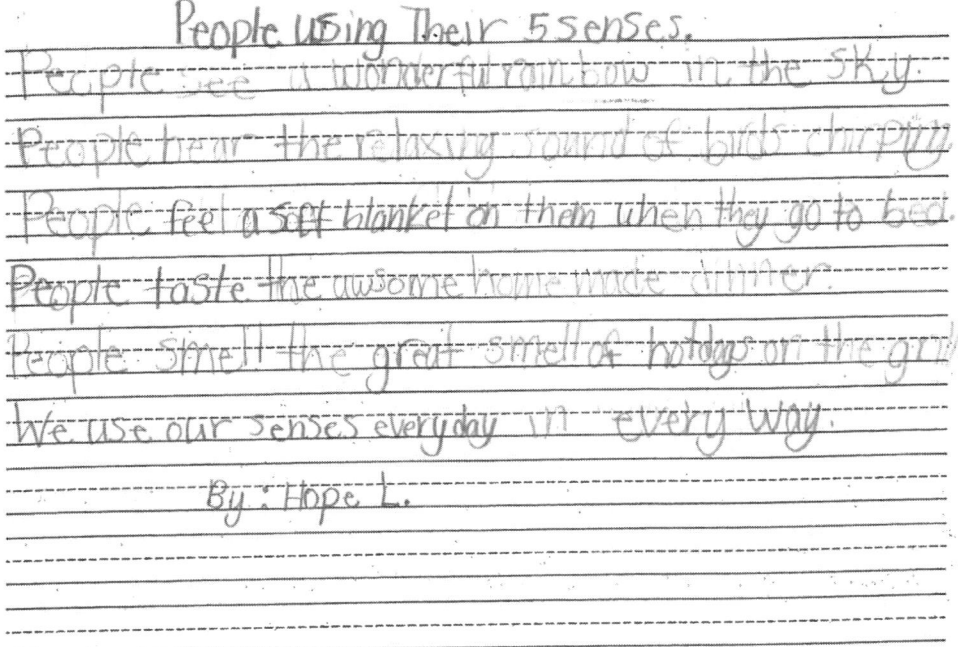

People using Their 5 senses.

People see a wonderful rainbow in the sky.

People hear the relaxing sound of birds chirping.

People feel a soft blanket on them when they go to bed.

People taste the awsome home made dinner.

People smell the great smell of hotdogs on the grill.

We use our senses everyday in every way.

By: Hope L.

Figure 8.4. Five Senses Poem

Writing Sentences

L.1.1, L.2.1, L.3.1

Have the students write an idea or two about people and use that information to complete the sentence "Because . . ." then draw an illustration depicting what they think people do. Use the following phrase as a starter for the class poem. See appendix A for a blank sample.

> When *we* think of all the people
> All those faces in *our* sight,
> If people are really colors,
> They must be more than
> Black or White.
> Because . . .

Book Review

W.K.1, W.1.1, W.2.1, W.3.1

Students will voice their opinions about the story. Begin by selecting a book students are familiar with. Then model the process of reviewing a book. For example, tell students what you liked about the book and why, what you least liked about the book and why, etc. Next, provide each student with a copy of the Book Review template (appendix A) to complete a review of the story. Have students use Audacity to record their book review.

Spotlight "It's All About Me"

SL.2.5, SL.3.5

Have students produce an All About Me episode for the class weekly, bi-weekly, or monthly radio show. In this episode, student groups will create segments using MP3 (Audacity) or MP4 (video) digital files to (1) report a glimpse of being proud of who they are and (2) share.

MEXICAN AMERICAN
The Pot That Juan Built by Nancy Andrews-Goebel (2002)
Grade Levels: K–3
Themes: Environment and Culture, Pottery, Mexico

Summary:

Andrew-Goebel's rhythmical use of language works in harmony with the beautiful and delightful art work by Diaz, a Caldecott winner. They tell a story of Juan Quezada, one of the well-known Mexican potters who uses ancient methods and natural materials for his pottery making.

Historical Information:

Mexican American history is a complicated and controversial subject. Current discourse about Mexican citizenship in the United States has its origins in early American history. Prior to the United States's push for western expansion, the Spanish, a large influence on indigenous cultures, had colonized much of the lands along the Gulf of Mexico.

LITERACY ACTIVITIES

Getting to Know Mexico

RI.K.1, RI.1.1, RI.2.1, RI.3.1, W.K.2, W.1.2, W.2.2, W.3.2

Tell students that the story they are about to listen to or read is located in Mexico. Use an app, a map, Google Earth, or a globe to locate Mexico. Point out that it shares a border with the United States. Then have the students Use the Internet or an app, or a map to find the following:

- The state of Chihuahua in the north
- Sierra Madre Mountains
- Mata Ortiz
- Palanganas River

Writing an Ad

RL.K.1, RL.1.1, RL.2.1, RL.3.1, SL.K.1, SL.1.1, SL.2.1, SL.3, W.K.7, W.1.7, W.2.7, W.3.7

Bring in newspaper and/or magazine advertisements about toys, food, clothes, etc. Discuss the message the ad is sending to the reader. Then have students work in pairs or small groups to write an ad (see figure 8.5) for the pottery of

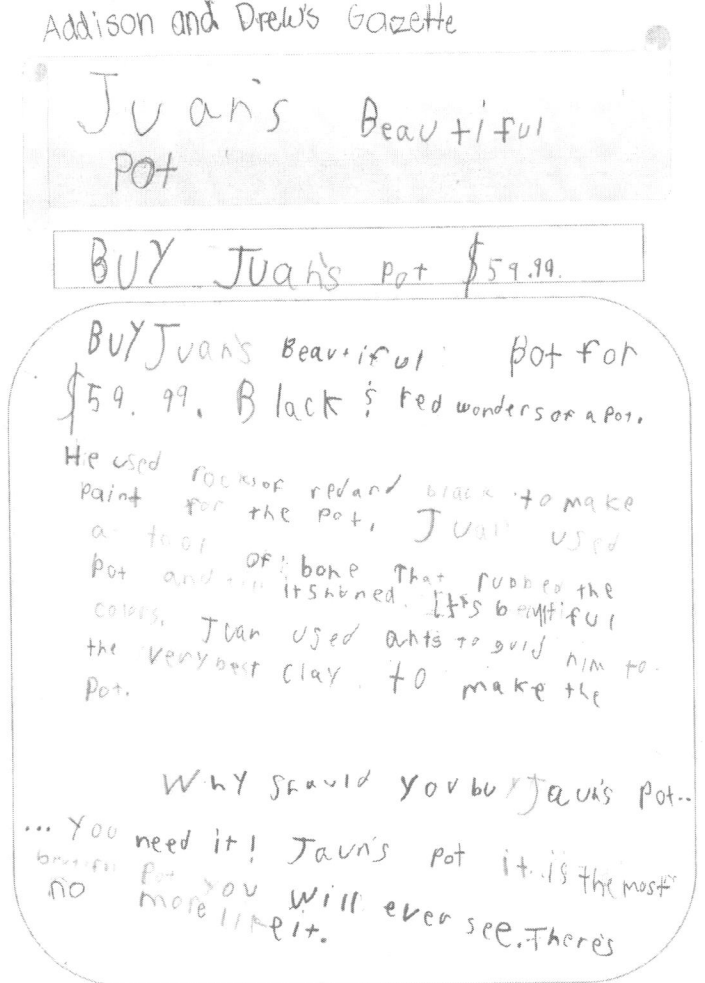

Figure 8.5. Writing an Ad

Juan Quezada. Tell students they can reread the poem to find ideas for promoting his work. For example, an ad might focus on the fact that he uses only natural resources for his materials.

Sentence Sequence

RL.1.2, RL.2.2, RL.3.2

Use the Sentence Sequence Activity (appendix A) to make several copies of the poem. Then cut out the sentences and rearrange them in a different order. Have students work in pairs or small groups to read and rearrange the poem in the correct order to retell the poem.

Identifying Poetic Forms

RL.K.5, RL.1.5, RL.2.5, RL.3.5

Use the poem in the book to teach or review poetic forms such as alliteration, metaphor, repetition, and onomatopoeia. For example:

- alliteration: "that flickered and flared"
- metaphor: "sausage of clay"
- repetition: point out how the lines of the poem are repeated on each page
- onomatopoeia: "crackling flames so sizzling hot"

Writing Poetic Forms

RL.K.1, RL.1.1, RL.2.1, RL.3.1, SL.K.1, SL.1.1, SL.2.1, SL.3.1, W.K.7, W.1.7, W.2.7, W.3.7

Students will work in small groups to reread the book and identify the poetic forms. Next, have each group add their own version to the poem by using any of the forms listed above. Then create a class book titled "Our Class Poetic Works." Use GarageBand or Windows Movie Maker to enhance the project.

Spotlight Mexico

SL.2.5, SL.3.5

Have students produce a Mexican American episode for the class weekly, bi-weekly, or monthly radio show. In this episode, student groups will create segments using MP3 (Audacity) or MP4 (video) digital files to (1) report a glimpse of Mexico's geography, history, and culture and (2) share the summary of book(s) from Mexico.

I Love Saturdays y Domingos by Alma Ada Flor (2002)
Grade Levels: PK–3
Themes: Grandparents, Heritages, Birthday Celebrations, Family

Summary:

This story parallels the joy of a little girl's weekends as she spends time with her English-speaking and Spanish-speaking grandparents. The author introduces the reader to both English and Spanish. Children with the same or similar backgrounds would easily connect to the theme of this book.

Historical Information:

When the Spanish left their territories in the New World, Mexico laid claim to where much of Southern California, Colorado, Nevada, New Mexico, Arizona, Utah, Wyoming, and Texas is today.

Unfortunately for Mexico, the freedom from Spanish control left the country weak and unstable. This made the conquering and absorption of land by the United States largely uncontested. The native Mexican citizens residing in these territories, found themselves in the awkward position of either leaving or assimilating.

Today's issues revolve around new waves of immigration from Mexico and other Hispanic countries. This is a hot topic and will continue to be so until a reasonable solution can be created.

LITERACY ACTIVITIES

Making Connections with Grandparents

RL.K.1, RL.1.1, RL.2.1, RL.3.1, RL.K.9, RL.1.9, RL.2.9, RL.3.9

Tell students that the girl in the story visits her two sets of grandparents on weekends. Her grandparents are of different ethnic backgrounds. Ask students to think about and describe the similarities and differences of their two sets of grandparents. Record students' responses on chart paper or a SmartBoard. Then tell students to listen to or read the story to find out about the similarities and differences of the little girl's grandparents.

Vocabulary

L.K.4, L.1.4, L.2.4, L.3.4

Using the word sort template (appendix A), have students cut and sort words according to languages. Then ask students to match the words according to meaning. For example,

Sunday (domingos), Grandpa (Abuelito), Grandma (Abuelita), Hi (Hola), sweetheart (hijita), How are you? (como estas?), come (ven), one (uno), two (dos), three (tres), four (cuatro), five (cinco), six (seis), seven (siete), etc. Then have students create their own English/Spanish dictionary using a World Language or Native Language app.

Using Self-Monitoring

RL.K.1, RL.1.1, RL.2.1, RL.3.1

Use think-aloud to model the self-monitoring strategy by reading the first two pages of the story. Stop at challenging words and illustrate the clarifying process.

First, write the word you don't know followed by a question mark. Next, think and write. At this point, think about strategies you can use to help clarify the word then write the strategy. For example, (1) read on, using context clues; (2) reread the sentence; (3) try using other clues; and (4) ask someone. Then use the strategy to find the solution. Finally, write the solution and continue reading.

Have students work in pairs or small groups as they read and provide them with a copy of Clarifying Words (appendix A).

Visualizing Strategy

RL.K.1, RL.1.1, RL.2.1, RL.3.1, W.K.1, W.1.1, W.2.1, W.3.1

Students will develop and build the comprehension strategy of visualizing. Discuss with students that good readers visualize or paint pictures of the text in their head as they read. Read any page(s) aloud to students two or three times. After reading, have students draw the image they saw in their head. Check students' images and check for comprehension. Allow students time to share.

Spotlight Influential Hispanic Americans

SL.2.5, SL.3.5

Have students produce an episode on Hispanic Heritage (http://www.time forkids.com/news/celebrating-hispanic-heritage/171181) for the class weekly, bi-weekly, or monthly radio show. In this episode, student groups will create segments using MP3 (Audacity) or MP4 (video) digital files to (1) report a glimpse of influential Hispanic Americans and (2) share.

RELATED APPS AND WEB RESOURCES

Apps for North America

- *Changing America:* Americans reacted to the Emancipation Proclamation in different ways. With Changing America: To Be Free, you can discover firsthand accounts of individual circumstances and reactions.
- *Black History People:* Discover all the facts about the inspirational lives and achievements of Rosa Parks, Martin Luther King Jr., Harriet Tubman, and other famous and noteworthy black people.
- *Black History Inventors:* The Black History Inventors reference includes many amazing individuals, some who have received U.S. patents.
- *African American Studies:* Read free African American studies books.
- *Native Language App:* Vision Maker Media's Native Language app is a great way for children and adults to learn different Native words from across Indian Country.
- *Native American Wisdom Deck:* This collection of Native American wisdom features the thoughts of Chief Joseph, Sitting Bull, Black Elk, Ohiyesa, and others on Native American ways of living, learning, and dying.
- *Native American Mythology:* Learn about mythology while playing a fun game of trivia.
- *Mexican Kids Songs and Rhymes:* Over eighty children's songs and rhymes that are popular in Mexico, presented in their original Spanish language and with translations into English.

North America—African American

For Teachers:

Federal
Resources for
Educational
Excellence

http://free.ed.gov/
   U.S. history topics ranging from business/work, famous people, government, movements, and other history studies.

Smithsonian Education

http://www.smithsonianeducation.org/educators/resource_library/african_american_resources.html

Black History Month calendar, Art and Life of William Johnson, aviators, National Museum of African American History and Culture (NMAAHC), highlights from SIRIS, etc.

Commissioner of Education's African American History Task Force

http://afroamfl.org/

Links to a wealth of rich resource sites for teachers like the African American Registry, African American History Workshop, African American classical music, Enchanted Learning, etc.

Teachervision

http://www.teachervision.fen.com/black-history-month/teacher-resources/6602.html

Has educational videos, slideshows, printables for K–12, language arts activities, math, etc.

Scholastic

http://teacher.scholastic.com/africanamericanheritage/

Resources and tools, strategies and ideas, books and authors, and lessons.

Learn NC

http://www.learnnc.org/lp/pages/774

Beyond Black History Month. Lesson plans, learning materials, and curriculum standards.

National Museum of African American History and Culture

http://www.nmaahc.si.edu/

Professional development workshops and seminars for educators. Mostly on-site, but some online seminars on different topics regarding African American history and/or culture.

The Dusable Museum of African-American History

http://www.dusablemuseum.org/

Love it! Educational programs, lesson plans, making history alive, storytelling, and "Penny Cinema."

Black Youth Project Research

http://research.blackyouthproject.com/byp-presents/teacher-resources/

In addition to the Black Youth Project Curriculum, the Teacher Resource page encompasses curriculum/lesson plans, professional development training programs, and tools that enrich teachers' instructional time covering issues of race, gender, class, and sexuality.

American Legacy Magazine

http://www.americanlegacymag.com/lesson-plans/

This site offers curriculum, including a Teacher's Starter Kit, regarding black history in music, pioneering women, politics, etc.

Examining African American Culture Through the Use of Children's Literature

http://www.yale.edu/ynhti/curriculum/units/1997/2/97.02.05.x.html

Full curriculum on the use of children's literature for examining black culture.

A–Z Teacher Stuff

http://www.atozteacherstuff.com/Themes/Black_History/

For grades 3 through 8. Covers lesson plans for cultural and historical moments.

Reading Rockets

http://www.readingrockets.org/calendar/blackhistory/
Writers recommended children's books, activities in the classroom, PBS programs, etc.

For Students:

PBS for Kids

http://pbskids.org/aaworld/
African American World. Games, e-cards, and youth social networking.

Nick Jr.

http://www.nickjr.com/black-history/
Very interactive site with online flashcards, coloring pages, etc. (for Black History Month).

Brown Baby Reads

http://www.brownbabyreads.com/
Cocoa Kids coming soon! An interactive literacy website featuring African American children and children's books.

North America—American Indian

For Teachers:

Federal Resources for Educational Excellence

http://free.ed.gov/
A vast collection of essays, pictures, and other resources for learning about Native American culture.

American Indians and Native Americans

http://www.teachervision.fen.com/native-american-heritage
-month/teacher-resources/6648.html#ixzz2rodjgvgx
Look here for lessons, activities, and printables on Native American life and culture. Use these resources to teach students of all ages about the colonization of America from a different perspective. You'll find great educational resources for Thanksgiving and Native American Heritage Month in November. There are also plenty of activities to use throughout the year for music, drama, art, and language arts.

*Education
World*

http://www.educationworld.com/a_special/black_history.shtml
Site for teachers and administrators, with lesson plans, technology, professional development, etc.

Teacher's First

http://www.teachersfirst.com/spectopics/nativeamericans.cfm
Outstanding site that includes Smartboard lessons, multimedia books, and videos for diverse topics centering around Native American culture and history. Sorted according to grade level.

*Learn NC
(American
Indians)*

www.learnnc.org/lp/pages/2778
Lesson plans, learning materials, curriculum standards, readings, and multimedia.

*Teacher's
Guide*

http://www.theteachersguide.com/nativeamericans.html
Native American lesson plans and ideas.

*American
Indian Games*

http://www.ndstudies.org/resources/activites/aind/AI-games.html
Games that can be played in the classroom or on the playground. The challenge to each student is to research and play more American Indian games, particularly ones played by the American Indians of North Dakota.

Scholastic

http://www.scholastic.com/teachers/student-activities
Student activities include science and writing for different age groups.

For Students:

*DLTKG's
for Kids*

http://www.dltk-kids.com/world/native/
Crafts for kids ages two to four.

WART Games

http://www.wartgames.com/themes/nativeamericans.html
Games, puzzles, and stories about Native Americans.

*American
Indian Library
Association*

http://ailanet.org/activities/american-indian-youth-literature
-award/
Site regarding American Indian youth literature.

TIME for Kids

http://www.timeforkids.com/search/site/american%20indian
This is compilation of videos, interviews, book recommendations,
etc., for the enhancement of learning for Native American children.

NORTH AMERICA—MUSCOGEE-CREEK TRIBE

For Teachers:

*Muscogee/
Creek Tribe*

http://www.legendsofamerica.com/na-creek.html
Native American Legends: The Muscogee (Creek) Nation.
Background information on the Muscogee (Creek) Nation.

For Students:

*Creek Indian
Fact Sheet*

http://www.bigorrin.org/creek_kids.htm
Native American Facts for Kids was written for young people
learning about the Muscogee Creeks for school or homeschooling
reports.

NORTH AMERICA—BIRACIAL

For Teachers:

Mixed Race
Identity
Development

http://www.mixedracestudies.org/wordpress/?Tag=sociology
-compass

Teaching and learning guide for multiracial Americans. Sociology-oriented articles that encompass a variety of topics regarding engrafting multiracial into multiculturalism.

Multiracial Sky

http://www.multiracialsky.com/community.html

Site contains information on the emotional impact and identity issues surrounding biracial people such as hair and skin. Includes resources for helping teachers and staff understand and properly support multiracial families.

Multiracial
Resources

http://www.robynochs.com/academia/teaching.html

Various websites and information regarding associations and organizations for transracially adopted children and interracial families. The site was created by Professor Robyn Ochs.

Articles and Journals

For Teachers:

Serving
Biracial and
Multiethnic
Children
and Their
Families—A
Video
and Early
Childhood

http://www.mixedheritagecenter.org/index.php?Itemid=29&id=902&option=com_content&task=view

http://www.mixedracestudies.org/wordpress/?Tag=is-that-your
-child-thought-in-full-color

This is a blog by parents of biracial children of different nation-
alities to support, inform, and encourage one another.

*Thought in Full
Color*

For Students:

http://www.readingrockets.org/article/creating-podcasts-your
-students

A step-by-step tutorial for teachers on how to create podcasts
with their students.

*Reading
Rockets*

http://freestoriesforkids.com/tales-for-kids/values-and-virtues/
stories-about-love

Stories for kids about love, including a short story about the love
of family.

Stories of Love

Mexican American

For Teachers:

http://www.loc.gov/teachers/classroommaterials/presentationsand
activities/presentations/immigration/mexican.html

This site covers a lot of cultural issues regarding Mexican mi-
gration into the United States, such as land loss, perceptions and
misconceptions, depression, and the struggle for survival, etc.

*Library of
Congress*

http://www.smithsonianeducation.org/educators/resource_library/
hispanic_resources.html

The Hispanic Heritage Teaching Resources section offers some
download information regarding Hispanic Heritage Month, Bra-
cero Program, Carnival Celebrations, etc.

*Smithsonian
Education*

http://www.ericdigests.org/2000-4/mexican.htm

This is a journal with links to sites that would be very useful in
pulling together a study.

*Cultural
Resources
for Mexican
American
Education*

For Students:

TIME for Kids

http://www.timeforkids.com/search/site/mexican
   This is compilation of videos, interviews, book recommendations, etc., for the enhancement of learning for Mexican children.

*Kids National
Geographic*

http://kids.nationalgeographic.com/kids/places/find/mexico/
   Facts, photos, geography, and related content.

9

SOUTH AMERICA

BRAZIL
***Brazil* by Elizabeth Weitzman (2008)**
Grade Levels: K–3
Themes: Culture, Language

Summary:

Brazil by Elizabeth Weitzman is a short chapter book that covers a wide variety of topics about Brazilian culture and life. Each chapter is about two pages long with the information laid out in colorful eye-catching designs. The photos used throughout the book are informative and interesting. For students studying Brazil, this book would be an ideal source of information.

Country Information:

Located in South America, the Federative Republic of Brazil possesses a significant amount of territory, comparable to the size of the United States. As a former territory of Portugal, Brazil has many cultural and historic roots in European history.

Unfortunately, this also includes participation in the trade of African slaves. The country has a long history of ethnic and racial diversity with several waves of immigration from all parts of the world (Japan, Germany, and Arab countries, to name a few), though Portuguese is the most commonly spoken language in the country. Interracial marriages exist at appreciable levels, but recent tensions between racial groups are becoming more common.

Most Brazilians who practice a religion follow Catholicism or Protestantism. However, variations of African religions are also found. Situated near the equator, Brazil's climate is mostly warm and tropical. Brazil is environmentally important because of its rainforests in the Amazon Basin. Agricultural products produced in Brazil include soybeans, rice, sugarcane, and citrus fruits. Unfortunately, Brazilian citizens struggle with unemployment and lower than ideal literacy rates (88 percent).

LITERACY ACTIVITIES

Compare and Contrast

RL.K.1, RL.1.1, RL.2.1, RL.3.1, RL.K.9, RL.1.9, RL.2.9, RL.3.9

Tell students that the story they are about to read or listen to takes place in Brazil. Then point out the location of Brazil using a globe, a map, or the Internet. Then have students compare things in Brazil and the United States. Use the topics that are provided within the chapters of the book. For example, school, television, getting around, families, and so forth. Provide each student with a copy of the compare and contrast chart (see figure 9.1). Then have students jot down a note explaining what the specific topic is like in Brazil as well as in their own lives.

Compare and Contrast
Brazil vs United States

Topic:	Brazil	United States
The Land	The land has Brazilian Highlands and the basin of the Amazon River.	There is 3,80 million square miles in the united States
Language	in brazil portuguese is the offical languadge. it is spoken by 99% of the population there.	people in america speak english & spanish mostly.
Transportation	They usually use road-rail-and water for their transportation	cars, boats, airplanes, trains, walk, & bikes and alot more!
Cultural Families	Maria Aux. liadora, Desren and Claudio V. Torres.	Aberhum Licons family george washingtons family & more
School	schools in brazil is maternal and jardimn	schools in america is indian hill, Mortin Luther King Jr. Elementary and more!
Food	food in brazil is shrimp, coconut milk, white rice and barbecued meat.	They like in america hotdogs, hamburgers, oreos, fris, pizza, potato chips, and more
Sports	Top sports in brazil is football (soccer) / Rugby, tennis, Judo, swimming, Gole and alot more.	sports in america is football, baseball, basketball, hockey, soccer, tennis, golf, wrestling, motorsports, and martial arts.

Figure 9.1.   Compare-Contrast

Questioning Strategy

RL.K.1, RL.1.1, RL.2.1, RL.3.1, SL.K.1, SL.1.1, SL.2.1, SL.3.1, W.K.7, W.1.7, W.2.7, W.3.7

The students will become naturally curious about things in Brazil, especially after they read the snippets that are offered for each chapter. The students will record their questions on Post-it notes and then place the notes inside their book. After completing the book, ask students to transfer the Post-its onto chart paper for class discussion. Allow time to research unanswered questions on the Internet.

Brazilian Vocabulary

L.2.3, L.3.3, L.K.4, L.1.4, L.2.4, L.3.4

Every culture has vocabulary that is unique to it. In this book, *Brazil*, there are several words that could be highlighted. The teacher should prepare a list of possible words and also allow the students to create their own list of words that they would like to better understand after the reading of the text.

From the list of words, students should each choose ten words to investigate. A possible selection of words may include *drought, favela, gauchos, novellas, swap, futebol, farofa, juninhas*, etc. The students can use this text and other texts about Brazil, dictionaries, encyclopedias, and the Internet to find definitions for their words.

To record the vocabulary, fold a piece of 11 × 17 paper in half lengthwise, making a tent. Then cut the top flap so that there are ten flaps to write the vocabulary word on and the matching definition underneath.

Writing Activity: *I want to _____ when I visit Brazil.*

W.K.1, W.1.1, W.2.1, W.3.1, W.K.3, W.1.3, W.2.3, W.3.3

Students will pretend they are about to visit Brazil. Then they will complete the following prompt: "I want to _____ when I visit Brazil." Students may write about what they would like to eat or any major highlights they are looking forward to seeing or doing. Students may choose something they have heard or read about in the text or learned about during their investigation of Brazil through one of the previously discussed activities.

Exploring Brazil

RI.K.1, RI.1.1, RI.2.1, RI.3.1, SL.K.4, SL.1.4, SL.2.4, SL.3.4, W.K.2, W.1.2, W.2.2, W.3.2

Students will be given the opportunity to work in small groups to prepare a PowerPoint presentation. The presentation should include the topic and information given from one of the subtopics of this book, *Brazil*. The presentation slides may vary depending on students' level of navigation skills and familiarity with this tool. Allow time for students to share this information with their peers.

Spotlight Brazil

SL.2.5, SL.3.5

Have students produce an episode on Brazil for the class weekly, bi-weekly, or monthly radio show. In this episode, student groups will create segments using MP3 (Audacity) or MP4 (video) digital files to (1) report a glimpse of Brazil's geography, history, and culture and (2) share the summary of book(s) from Brazil.

COLOMBIA
My Name Is Gabito **by Monica Brown (2007)**
Grade Levels: K–3
Themes: Imagination, Storytelling

Summary:
Gabriel "Gabito" Garcia Marquez is a celebrated writer. Author Monica Brown brings the powerful imagination and compassion of Gabito to life in this beautifully illustrated book. The story is told in English and Spanish. The writing prompts the reader to imagine along with Gabito. Readers who desire a more full account of Gabito's life will be delighted by the author's biography provided in the back.

Country Information:
The Republic of Colombia is the former territory of Spain. Prior to its independence from the Spanish government in the early 1800s, Colombia was part of a confederation of states with Venezuela, Ecuador, and Panama known as the "Viceroyalty of New Granada." Today Colombia has an independent government and enjoys a relatively thriving economy despite recent warfare. Colombia is the only country in South America to have coastline on both the Pacific Ocean and the Caribbean Sea.

Listed among Colombia's natural resources are emeralds and gold. Agricultural products include cut flowers, coffee, and shrimp. Colombians also enjoy relatively high literacy rates at almost 93 percent. However, because of different mandatory education policies between rural and urban areas, rural populations are less literate and spend less time in school.

LITERACY ACTIVITIES

Sequencing Important Events

RI.K.3, RI.1.3, RI.2.3, RI.3.3

Tell students that the story they are about to read or listen to takes place in Colombia. Then point out the location of Colombia using an app, Google Earth, a globe, a map, or the Internet. Then have students identify main events that lead Garcia Marquez to be an author. They will then put the events in order to show what lead up to the author's success. Some examples may be the places he went with his grandfather to tell stories, his pet parrot that talked and told stories, and so forth.

Be an Investigator

W.1.7, W.2.7, W.3.7, W.1.8, W.2.8, W.3.8

My Name Is Gabito is a book that tells the story about a famous author named Gabriel Garcia Marquez. The students will write a letter to an author of their choice asking how they became an author. They can ask things about what inspired them, what they love to write about, or who encouraged them to write. Students could also work in small groups as they develop a plan to interview someone they know who loves to write. They begin by writing possible interview questions. Next, they meet with the interviewee. Allow time for students to share their results.

Choral Reading

RF.K.4, RF.1.4, RF.2.4, RF.3.4

Have students listen as you read the story. After modeling, focus on the sentence "Can You Imagine?" (appendix A), which is repeated throughout the story. Next, reread the sentence and have the students echo it back to you. This will be followed by having the students chorally read the sentence to increase fluency and gain confidence. The repetition of this line will empower the students to become successful readers as they focus on expression and rate.

Describing Words

L.2.1, L.3.1

The author consistently uses juicy adjectives in the story. Ask the students to go on a word hunt to find some of these adjectives or describing words. Read the following sentence to the students: *"His father always let him dip his hands into the pitcher of water and lift out the **cold** and **crunchy** ice cubes."* Have students identify the adjectives that are in this sentence.

Can You Imagine Poem

W.K.3, W.1.3, W.2.3, W.3.3

Using the repetitive line in the story, "Can you imagine," the students will write their own Can You Imagine poem, starting each sentence with the words "Can you imagine." Then they will create their own story prompts of things they imagine in their own lives.

For an extension they can actually write about one of the things they ask the reader to imagine. Provide students with a blank copy of the Can You Imagine Poem Template (appendix A). The students will use a digital recording device to record their poems.

Spotlight Colombia

SL.2.5, SL.3.5

Have students produce an episode on Colombia for the class weekly, bi-weekly, or monthly radio show. In this episode, student groups will create segments using MP3 (Audacity) or MP4 (video) digital files to (1) report a glimpse of Colombia's geography, history, and culture and (2) share the summary of book(s) from Colombia.

PERU
Tomasino: A Child of Peru by Herve Giraud (2005)
Grade Levels: K–3
Themes: Culture, Family

Summary:
  In this story, the author gives a snapshot of the life of Tomasino, a young Quechuan Indian boy who lives in Peru. Color photos are used to depict the many things he does throughout the day.

Country Information:

The Republic of Peru has a long history, which began with the ancient civilization of the Incas. While many Peruvians are of mestizo ancestry, the largest minority group in Peru is still made up of indigenous populations. In addition to this, Peru is also home to several "uncontacted" indigenous tribes, meaning that there are still populations of people oblivious to the rest of the world. Peru is a unique combination of ancient and modern traditions.

Peru is geographically significant not only because it has rainforests but also because it shares control over the source of the Amazon River with Bolivia. Peru's climate is warm and tropical, which allows for a variety of products to be cultivated.

Peruvian agriculture includes asparagus, paprika, coffee, and bananas. Peruvians are primarily Spanish speaking. The country is also overwhelmingly Christian, with few other religions practiced. Literacy is high but noticeably higher for males (93 percent versus 82 percent for females).

LITERACY ACTIVITIES

KWL—South American Children

RL.K.1, RL.1.1, RL.2.1, RL.3.1, SL.K.1, SL.1.1, SL.2.1, SL.3.1

Show students the cover of the book. Tell students that this story takes place in Peru. Then point out the location of Peru using the Internet, an app, a map, Google Earth, or a globe.

Next, have the students fill out a KWL chart on what they know and want to know about children from South America and write their responses on chart paper or a SmartBoard. Later follow up with what they learned and chart responses in the "L" section. They may also make predictions about what they think about the schools in South America, what they eat, what they wear, etc., if their background knowledge on Peru is limited.

Things in Common

RL.K.9, RL.1.9, RL.2.9, RL.3.9

The student will make connections with Tomasino. They will need to give three examples of how they are alike and two examples about how they are different. Things to think about might be the food they eat, clothes they wear, sports they play, etc. A blank comparison chart is available in appendix A for the students.

Nonfiction Features

RI.K.5, RI.1.5, RI.2.5, RI.3.5, W.K.2, W.1.2, W.2.2, W.3.2

Students will explore the nonfiction features of this text. There is an example of a table of contents, photos, captions, a comparison, and a map. The students can see an example of each of these features and then create their own example in a Nonfiction Conventions book.

Vocabulary Development

L.K.4, L.1.4, L.2.4, L.3.4

There are many words that the students may not be familiar with in this informational text. Before reading, the teacher will lead a discussion about the vocabulary words, and then the students will engage in a matching activity on the SmartBoard in which they match the words with the correct definitions. The follow up will be to talk about the words within context while reading the story. The words that will be focused on are mountains, volcanoes, invigorating, language, harvested, catastrophe, and immense. (The teacher may add other words to this list.)

Spotlight Peru

SL.2.5, SL.3.5

Have students produce an episode on Peru for the class weekly, bi-weekly, or monthly radio show. In this episode, student groups will create segments using MP3 (Audacity) or MP4 (video) digital files to (1) report a glimpse of Peru's geography, history, and culture and (2) share the summary of book(s) from Peru.

VENEZUELA
Venezuela ABCs **by Sharon Kutz Cooper (2007)**
Grade Levels: K–3
Themes: Culture, Alphabets

Summary:

Sharon Kutz Cooper's book explores the unique beauty and traditions of Venezuela through use of the alphabet. For each letter in the alphabet Cooper cleverly integrates fascinating information about Venezuela. Colorful illustrations, a Spanish-English dictionary, and language and cultural resources make this book a wonderful teaching aid.

Country Information:

The Bolivarian Republic of Venezuela is a warm, tropical country home to the majestic Angel Falls, the world's tallest waterfall. The country has a long history with European powers, beginning with Spain. Venezuela was one of the countries in South America to be a part of the New Granada confederation.

Spanish is the official language, and the majority of practicing Venezuelans follow Roman Catholicism. Venezuela has a young population with almost half the citizens under the age of twenty-five. Literacy rates in Venezuela are very high, with school systems that require at least nine years of education.

Venezuela's main export is oil, which makes its economy vulnerable to the rapid rise and decline of the oil industry. The president has enacted a series of governmental reforms aimed at gaining larger control over the country's economy. Agricultural resources include corn, sorghum, rice, and fish. The United States is the largest consumer of Venezuela's exports.

LITERACY ACTIVITIES

KWLPlus

RL.K.1, RL.1.1, RL.2.1, RL.3.1

Show students the cover of the book. Tell students that this story takes place in Venezuela. Then point out the location of Venezuela using the Internet, a map, or a globe. Prior to reading the book, tell students they will be using KWL-Plus (Carr and Ogle 1987) to express what they know.

First, display the KWL chart and tell students that they will also take part in a writing activity to demonstrate what they have learned. Have the students list the things they already know about Venezuela in the "K" section. Then list the things they want to know about Venezuela to establish purpose for reading the book in the "W" section. After reading the book, list the things they have learned from the readings in the "L" section.

Finally, have students sort the information they listed in the "L" section. Tell students this sorted information will be used to assist each small group in writing about what they know.

Cultural Class Book

W.3.4, W.1.7, W.2.7, W.3.7

Each student in the class gets a letter of the alphabet. They need to research something that is important to American and Venezuelan culture or heritage that matches their assigned letter, which they will write in the box on the upper left-hand side of the paper (see figure 9.2). Students will also write a few sentences about their topic.

Tell students to draw a picture in the box below their sentences to describe what they chose for their letter. This lesson could include reviewing the writing process to begin writing all the way to "publishing" the class book.

Figure 9.2. Breanna

Alphabetizing Venezuelan Vocabulary

L.1.4, L.2.4, L.3.4, W.K.7, W.1.7, W.2.7, W.3.7

After reading the text once or twice, encourage student to make a list of words they want to know more about that they heard or read in the story. Come together as a class to compile a large list of vocabulary from this story. Allow students to work in small groups to define each of their words on a 4 × 5 index card or provide students access to the app Evernote Peek for creating digital flashcards.

After all of the words have been investigated, bring all of the students together to share their findings. Students can then work as a class to alphabetize the vocabulary words they explored. During another session the teacher will provide the students with a copy of the words they investigated that can be cut out for them to practice alphabetizing independently. See appendix A for a copy of the blank cards for alphabetizing the vocabulary words.

Letters of the Alphabet

RF.K.4, RF.1.4, RF.2.4, RF.3.4

Have students each read one of the letter pages of the book. The students will enjoy practicing reading their page to record as they improve their reading expression and fluency, just as much as they will enjoy listening to both their peers and their own voice on the recording of the story. Students could use this digital recording to share with another class or a class of younger students.

Spotlight Venezuela

SL.2.5, SL.3.5

Have students produce an episode on Venezuela for the class weekly, biweekly, or monthly radio show. In this episode, student groups will create segments using MP3 (Audacity) or MP4 (video) digital files to (1) report a glimpse of Venezuela's geography, history, and culture and (2) share the summary of book(s) from Venezuela.

RELATED APPS AND WEB RESOURCES

Apps for South America

- *South America:* South America is an educational app used in schools throughout the world to help students learn the names, locations, flags, capitals, and geographical shapes of the countries in South America.
- *Basic Sequencing Skills:* Put pictures, alphabets, and numbers in a sequence. This app with its multiple levels is like a workbook to exercise little minds.
- *Story Boarder:* Build and share photo story boards, snapping shots from your camera or selecting them from your device and adding them in a sequence.
- *StoryBoards:* Your students don't need any drawing ability to use this simple, dedicated story boarding app. Hundreds of character models and props are available to compose each shot.
- *Alphabetical Order:* Practice putting the letter blocks into alphabetical order.
- *Brazil Animal Adventures:* Animal Adventures for Kids is a gorgeous app filled with fun animations for children to learn about the animals of Brazil.

WEBSITES

Brazil

For Teachers:

http://resources.primarysource.org/content.php?Pid=127542&sid=1096220

This site contains an online curriculum, websites, books, film, art, and news for instructing and learning Brazilian culture.

Primary Source Educating for Global Understanding

http://countries.mrdonn.org/brazil.html

Activities and learning modules, lesson plans, games, music, videos, clip art, etc.

Mr. Donn (Brazil)

For Students:

http://kids.nationalgeographic.com/kids/places/find/brazil/
Facts, photos, geography, and related content.

*Kids National
Geographic*

http://www.factmonster.com/ipka/A0930059.html
   This would be useful for older students seeking just facts about Brazil.

Fact Monster

http://www.exploreandmore.org/world/default.htm
   Interactive map with multiple country games, fast facts, and local scenery.

*Cultures
for Kids*

Colombia

For Teachers:

http://www.everyculture.com/Bo-Co/Colombia.html
   This site has a little history, geography, demography, etc., to give a background on Colombian culture and history, including information regarding urbanization, architecture, and use of space.

Every Culture

For Students:

http://kids.nationalgeographic.com/kids/places/find/colombia/
Facts, photos, geography, and related content.

*Kids National
Geographic
Colombia*

https://kidskonnect.com/
   Extensive multiple links to other sites regarding weather, travel, culture and history, the capital city, volcanoes.

Kids Connect

Britannica Kids

http://kids.britannica.com/comptons/article-198905/Colombia

This site has information best used for older children regarding land and climate, people and culture, ethnic groups, language and religion, economy, government, and more.

Peru

For Teachers:

Teacher Zone— Achievements and Challenges of Peru

http://www.worldtrek.org/odyssey/teachers/perulessons.html

This unit is intended to focus on some of those aspects of Peruvian life and history that are of great significance to understanding the people of Peru and their situation today. By using or adapting the core lessons and activities, your students will learn about the Peruvian culture. The site is linked in outline format.

For Students:

TIME for Kids

http://www.timeforkids.com/search/site/peru

This is a compilation of videos, interviews, book recommendations, etc., for the enhancement of learning for or about Peruvian kids and culture.

Kids National Geographic

http://kids.nationalgeographic.com/kids/places/find/peru/

Facts, photos, geography, and related content.

Venezuela

For Teachers:

Spark Enthusiasm

http://www.sparkenthusiasm.com/venezuela_resources.html

PowerPoint and Animation, leaders of Spanish speaking countries, monetary units, famous Hispanics, ready-to-go resources, movies in Spanish, recommended websites, and more!

For Students:

Fact Monster

http://www.factmonster.com/ipka/A0108140.html

This site deals with facts regarding this city, geography, history, government, land, and population. Great site if a student needs just facts.

Britannica Kids

http://kids.britannica.com/comptons/article-209776/Venezuela

More encyclopedic information regarding culture, ethnic groups, education, social welfare, economy, religion, etc.

Atoz Kids Stuff

http://www.embavenezus.org/?Pagina=kids.venezuela/intro.htm& titulo=Venezuela%20for%20Kids

This site repeats more of the same information, but includes a link called The Embassy, which takes you to folklore and traditions and includes pictures of Christmas, festivals, etc.

Spark Enthusiasm

http://www.sparkenthusiasm.com/Student_Resources.html

Videos, recommended sites, proficiency improvement, vocabulary, culture, etc.

Misc.

Teacher's Corner

http://www.theteacherscorner.net/

Resources, lesson plans, worksheets, collaboration projects, lounge, and jobs.

Teaching Kids News

http://teachingkidsnews.com/2013/03/07/1-hugo-chavez-venuzuelan-president-dies/

This is a news-oriented blog for students, parents, and teachers. Includes in-class assignments.

Explore and More: A Children's Museum

http://www.exploreandmore.org/world/default.htm

Teacher resources for bringing other cultures into the classroom.

APPENDIX A

KWL Chart

what I *Know*	what I *Want* to know	what I *Learned*

KWL

Venn Diagram

Venn Diagram

Friendly Letter Template

DATE

GREETING:

BODY:

CLOSING AND SIGNATURE:

Friendly Letter

Story #1	Criteria	Story #2
	Characters Use the characters words, actions, and thoughts.	
	Setting when and where	
	Problem	
	Event	
	Event	

Story Elements

Sorting Descriptive Words

Think about how you see yourself as a person. Then sort words describing your character on the inside and outside.

My Invisible
Characteristics

My Visible
Characteristics

Activity 1: Basket of Bangles

Sorting Descriptive Words I

Using Descriptive Words

Think about how you see yourself as a person. Then write words describing your character traits.

My Character Traits

Write a sentence about yourself using some of your character traits.

Sorting Descriptive Words II

SOMETHING TO CROW ABOUT!

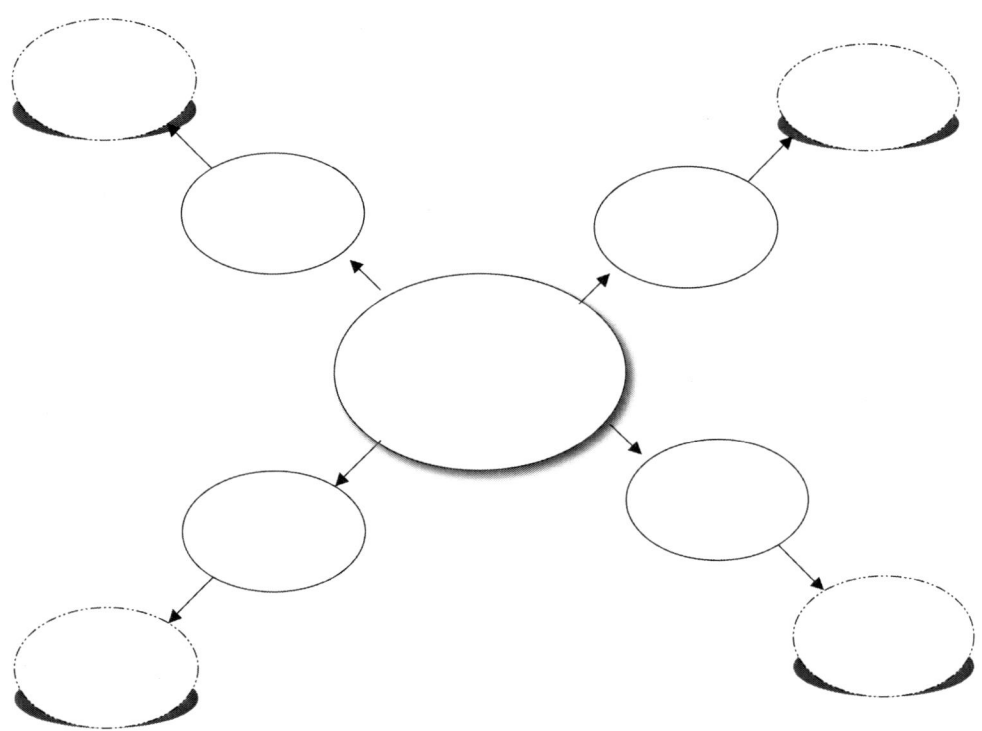

Something to Crow About 1

SOMETHING TO CROW ABOUT!

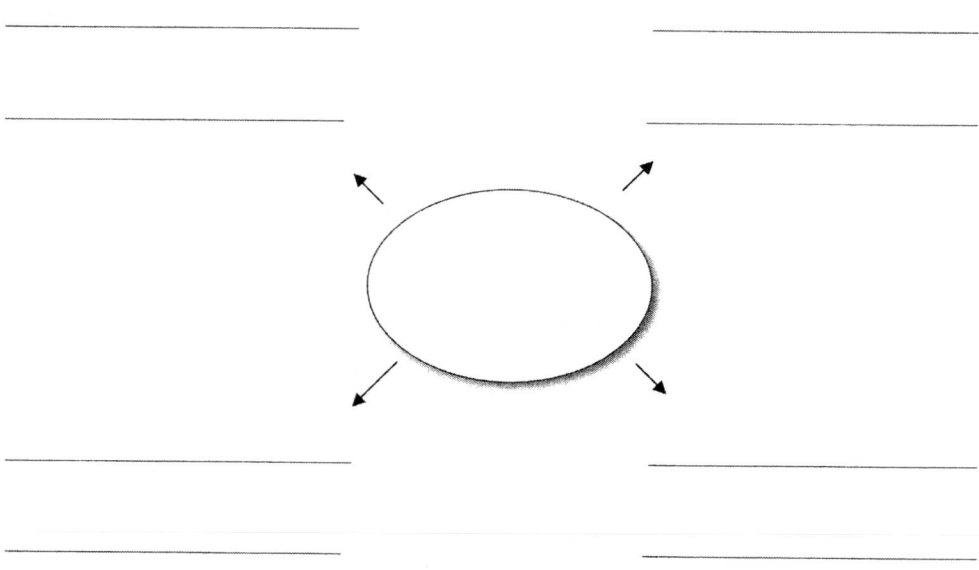

Activity 3: My Father's Shop

Something to Crow About II

:Fatuma's New Cloth

Writing a Friendship
Poem

Create an acrostic poem using your friend's name. Write each letter in his/her name in a top-to-bottom position. Use as many lines as needed.

_____ _____

_____ _____

_____ _____

_____ _____

_____ _____

_____ _____

_____ _____

_____ _____

Writing a Friendship Poem

Nelson Mandala's
Bio-Poem

Write a bio-poem about Nelson Mandala using the ll-line formula.

(First name)-
(Four adjectives that describe the person)
Son or Daughter of (your parents names)
Lover of (three different things that the person loves)
Who feels (three different feelings **and** when or where they are felt)
Who gives (three different things the person gives)
Who fears (three different fears the person has)
Who would like to see (three different things the person would like to see)
Who lives (a brief description of where the person lives)
-(last name)

Example:

Nelson
Brave, extraordinary, strong-minded, leader
Son of
Nelson Mandala's Bio Poem

Great Things about the U.S.!

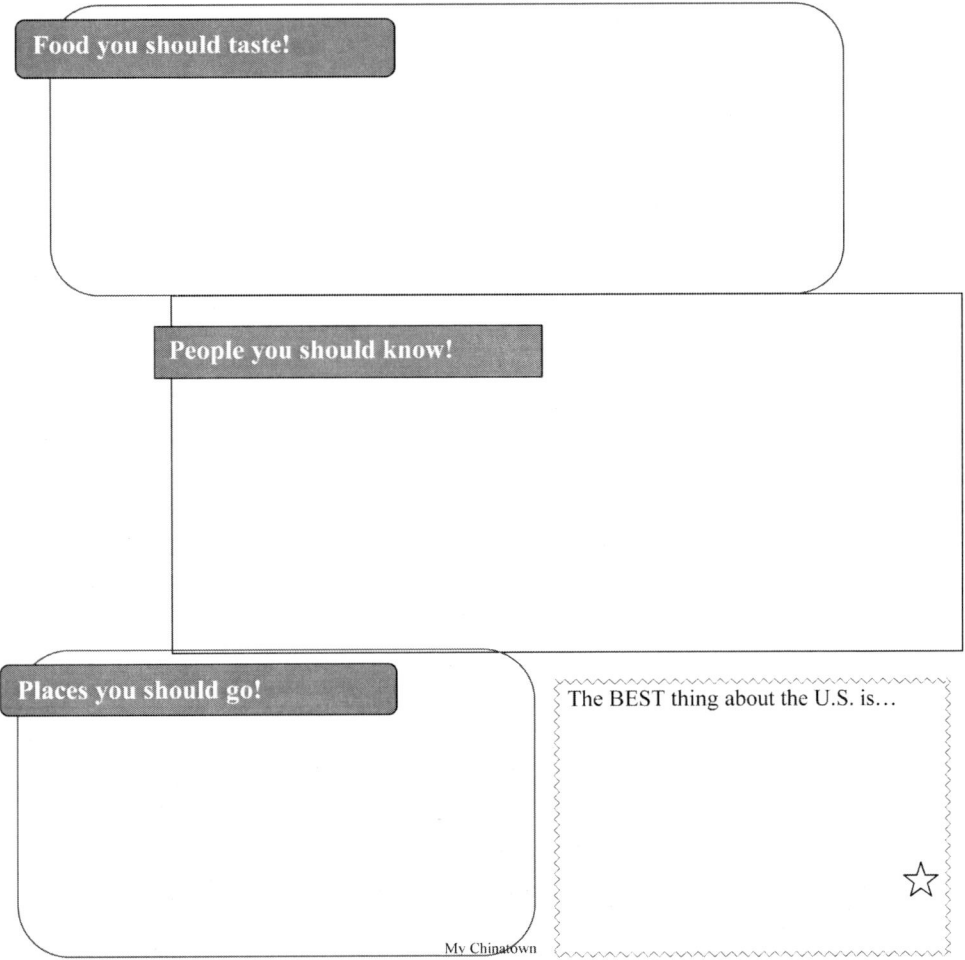

Food you should taste!

People you should know!

Places you should go!

The BEST thing about the U.S. is…

☆

My Chinatown

Great Things About the United States

What would I take with me?

Inside the suitcase, make a list of things you will take with you if you had only one day to pack.
Then write why you decided to take the things on your list with you.

My list:

Why would I take these things with me?

What Would I Take with Me?

Past and Present

PAST	PRESENT
Communication:	Communication:
Transportation:	Transportation:

Past and Present

My plan to bring people back to the Chinese Opera

Why is it important to keep Chinese Opera?

What will happen if the Chinese tradition disappears?

What will happen to the people below if Chinese Opera disappears?
Opera singers, directors and the crew.

People who make money by advertising and providing materials to make the set and dresses.

What are some ideas on how to bring back people to watch Chinese Opera?

My Plan to Bring People Back to the Chinese Opera

Create an advertisement using the information above.

A Song for Ba

Education or Tradition?

Benefits of Education

Benefits of Tradition

If I were Wei, I would choose _____ because

A Song for Ba

Education or Tradition?

My Chinatown

Good Readers Think!

Events	What I was thinking

Suki's Kimono

Good Readers Think

Kimono ("key-mo-no")

What did you learn from reading *Suki's Kimono?*

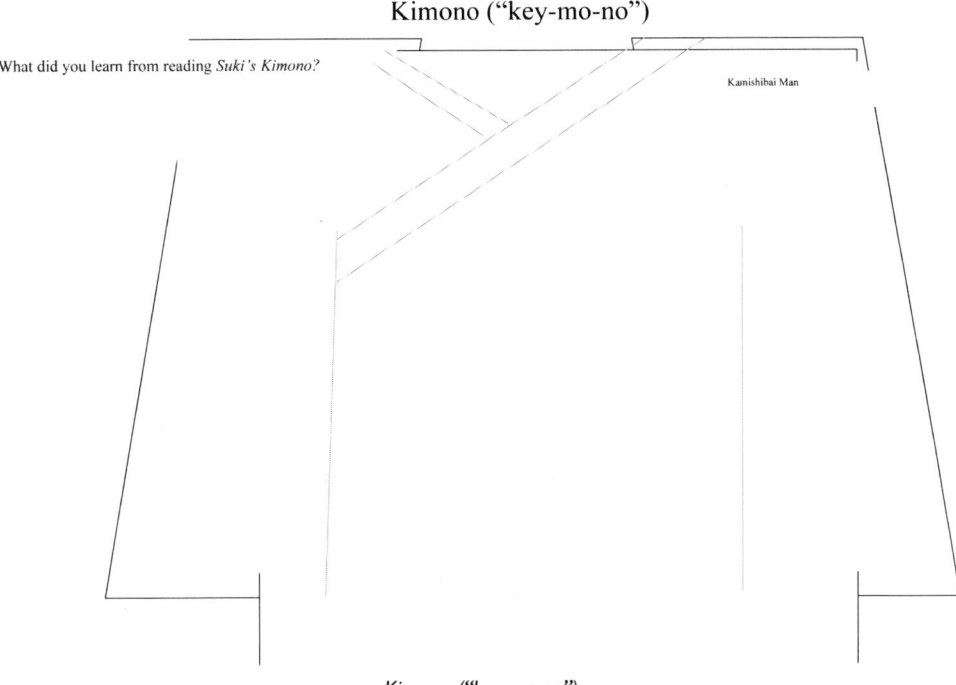

Kamishibai Man

Kimono ("key-mo-no")

Suki's Word Challenge
Suki's Word Challenge

Directions: Look at the pre-selected words. Say each word and place a check in the box to identify your level of word knowledge [have heard it, have seen it, know it.] Then write what you think the word means. Finally, use a dictionary or other sources to write what the word really means.
*You may write additional words during or after reading the story.

Word	I have heard it	I have seen it	I know it	I think it means	It really means

Suki's Kimono

Suki's Word Challenge

Changes in Jennifer's Feelings

Describe how Jennifer's feelings changed throughout the story.
<u>Why</u> was she feeling that way?

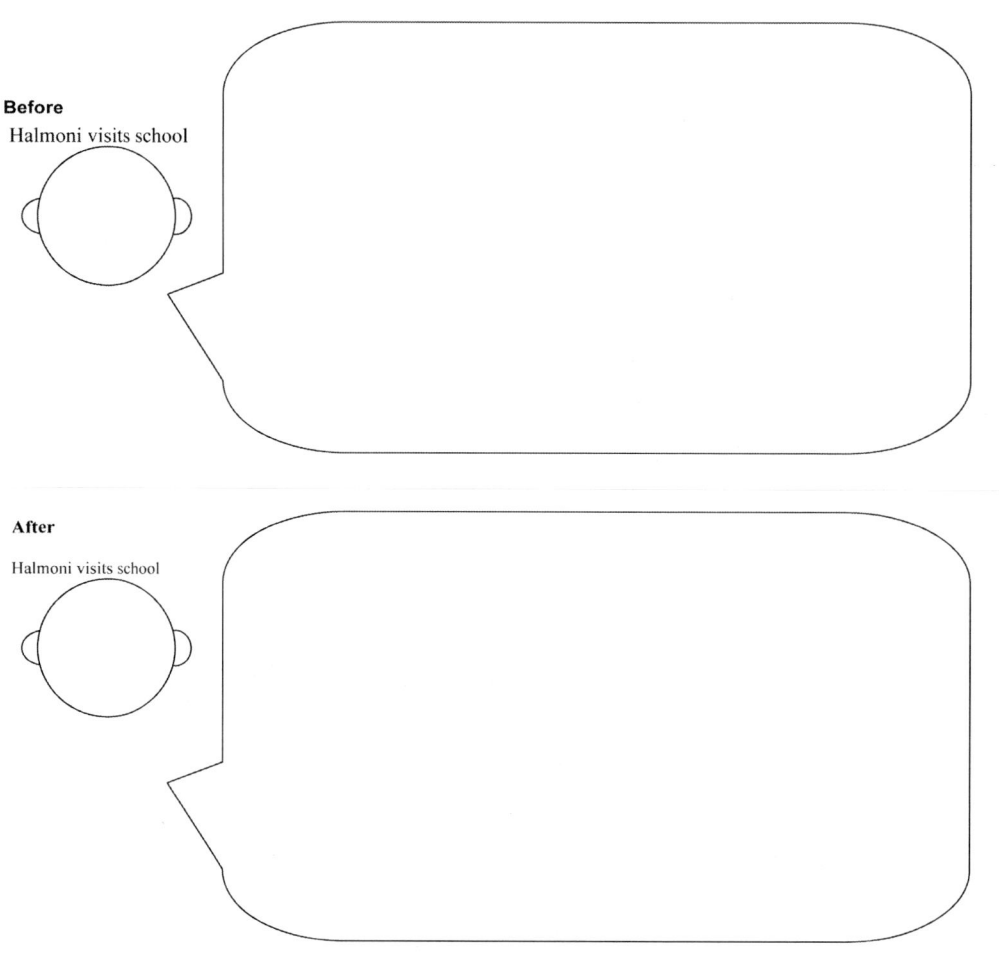

Before
Halmoni visits school

After

Halmoni visits school

Changes in Jennifer's Feelings

Halmoni's Day

Be a Culture Detective!

✎   Find things that show the Korean culture in the book.

✎   Compare and contrast with your own culture.

These are things that are **alike**.

These are things that are **different**.

Halmoni's Day

Be a Culture Detective

Steps to starting our own business!

Owners: _____   _____

_____   _____

_____   _____

Name of Business: _____

Step 1: What are our principles?

Step 2: What do we need to buy to start our business?

~Supply List~

Step 3: How much are we going to borrow from the bank? $_____

Step 4: How are we going to use our money? ~Our Plan~

Step 5: How much will we save?

Steps to Starting Our Own Business

The 4 Principles

Select one of the 4 Principles then write synonyms on the star describing how it will be met. Cut and glue onto a construction paper.

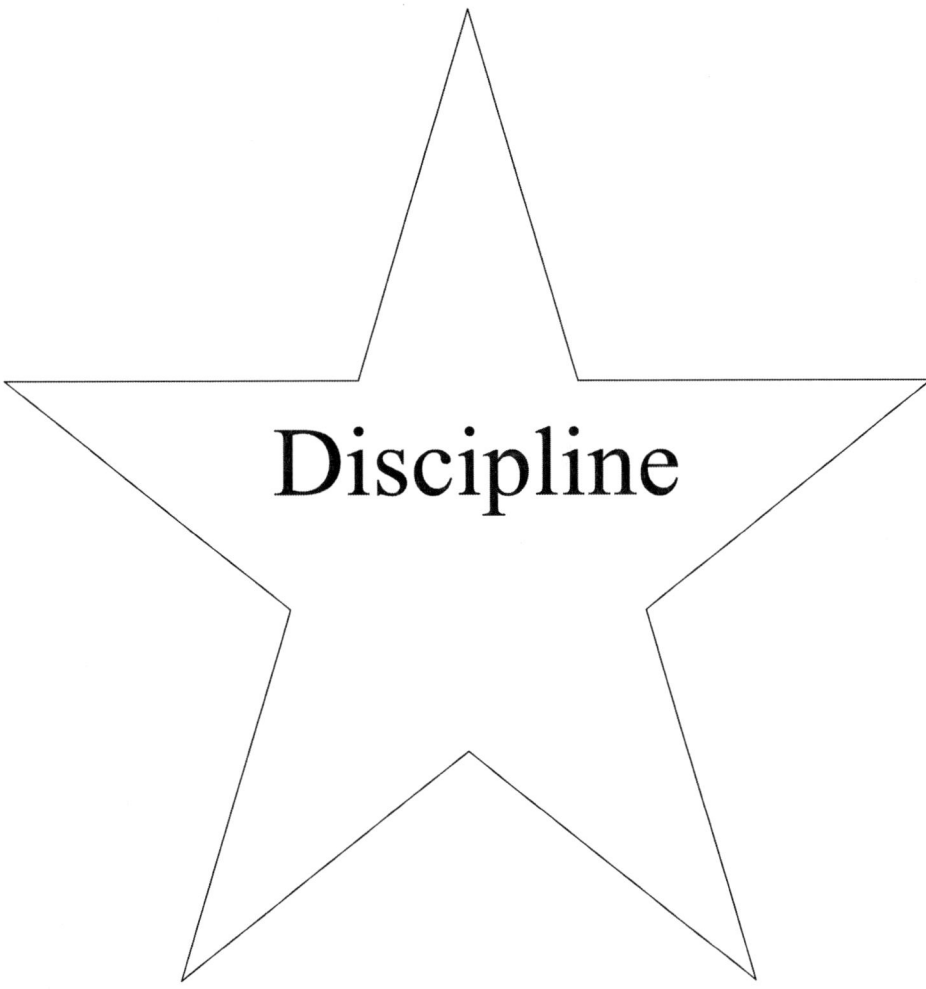

The Four Principles

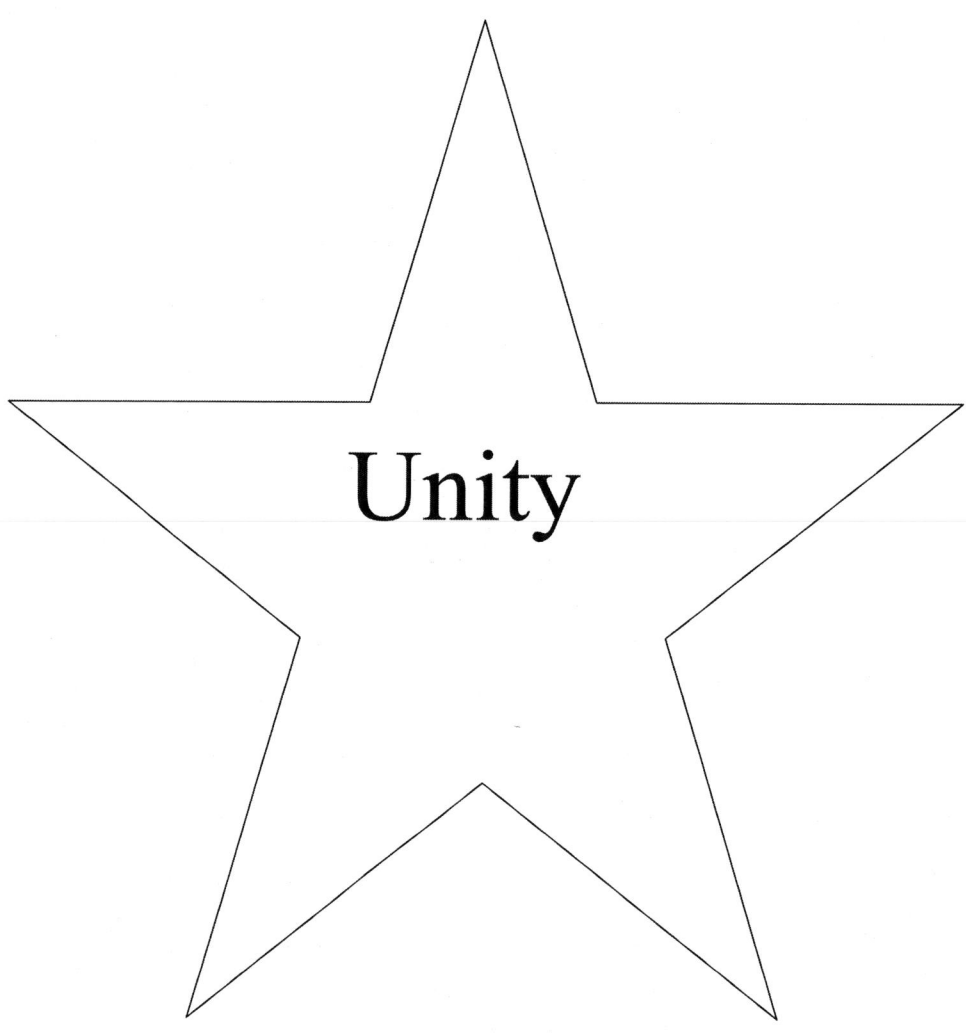

Unity

The Four Principles (continued)

Basket of Bangles

Courage

The Four Principles (continued)

Basket of Bangles

Hard Work

The Four Principles (continued)

Monsoon Rain in India
KWL Chart

what I *Know*	what I *Want* to know	what I *Learned*

Monsoon

Monsoon Rain in India (KWL)

Summarizing Monsoon

Read the story then write or dictate parts of the story by using one-sentence summaries. Cut and staple to make your miniature Monsoon book.

My Summary
Page ____

_____

_____

_____

_____

_____.

My Summary
Page ____

_____

_____

_____

_____

_____.

My Summary
Page ____

_____

_____

_____

_____

_____.

My Summary
Page ____

_____

_____

_____

_____

_____.

Summarizing Monsoon

Word Sort Template

Word Sort Template

Making a Postcard

Four Feet, Two Sandals

Making a Postcard

What does it take for a plant to grow?

What kind of environment is Facile trying to plant the tree for his new baby sister?

What happened to the seeds that he tried to plant?

What do you think seeds need in order to grow? What did Facile need?

The Recipe

How-to-Plant-and-Take-Care Recipe

Main dish (what I am trying to grow) _____

Circles of Hope

Ingredients (what do I need to plant this flower?)

Steps (how do I plant this flower?)

_____

How to Plant and Take Care Recipe

Plot Summary
Fold-up Book
(Cut then fold on dotted lines. Change the end of the story)

Author:

*Change the end of the story.

Rata-Pata-Scata-Fata: A Caribbean Story

Plot Summary Fold-Up Book

Feelings Chart

Events	Derrick	Colly
Mrs. Wong gave them some hooks		
By noon their snacks were gone.		
Colly fell down the muddy bank		

Fish for the Grand Lady

Feelings Chart

Predicting and Confirming Chart *with* Reasons

My predictions for the beginning, middle, and end of story.	I made this prediction because:	What really happened
Beginning		
Middle		
Middle		
End		

My Name Was Hussein

Predicting and Confirming Chart

Story Mapping

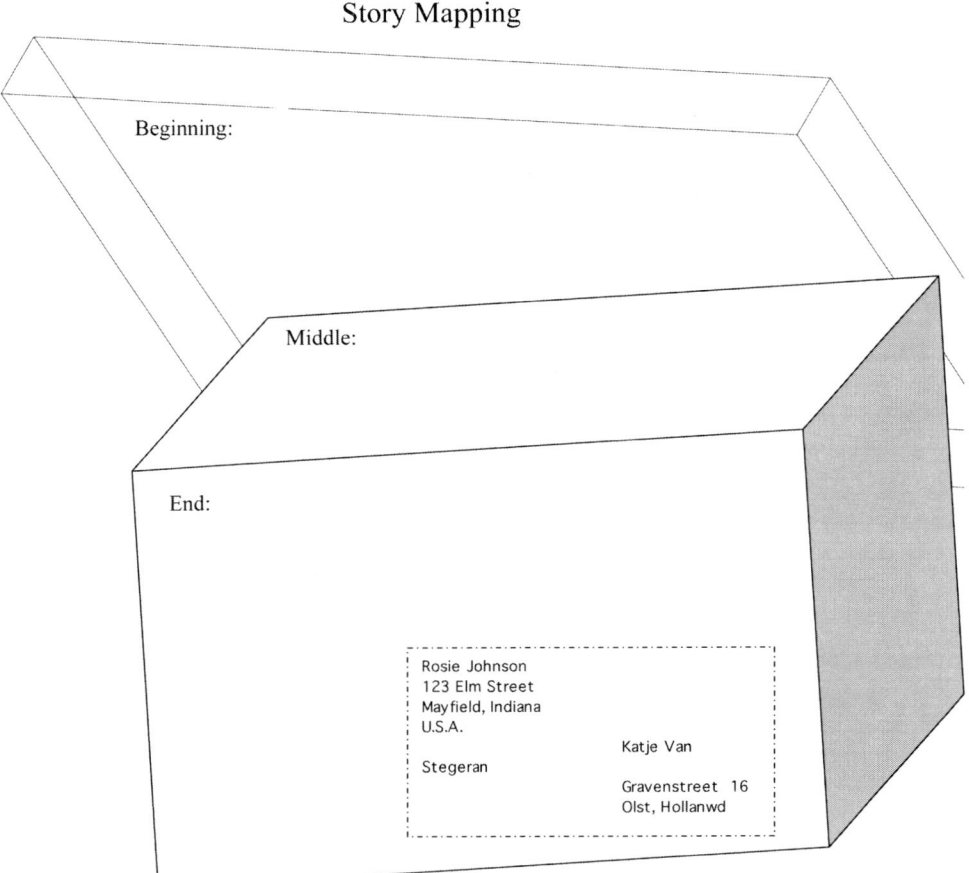

Beginning:

Middle:

End:

Rosie Johnson
123 Elm Street
Mayfield, Indiana
U.S.A.
                                        Katje Van

Stegeran

                                        Gravenstreet 16
                                        Olst, Hollanwd

Story Mapping

Matching Antonyms in Boxes for Katje

Words	Antonyms
Old	
Open	
Push	
Send	
Dark	

Matching Antonyms in Boxes for Katje

Anticipation Guides for *In English of Course*

Before Reading	Statements	After Reading
Agree Disagree		Agree Disagree
_____ _____	1. A new language is always easy to understand.	_____ _____
_____ _____	2. A new language is always easy to speak.	_____ _____
_____ _____	3. Being different is fun!	_____ _____
_____ _____	4. It's important to learn other languages.	_____ _____
_____ _____	5. The teacher provided Josephine with a good choice of words when helping her tell her story.	_____ _____

In English of Course

Anticipation Guides for In English, Of Course

LITERARY REPORT CARD

Astoria Elementary		
Student: Josephine		
G- Good S- satisfactory N- Needs to Improve		
Characteristic	**Grade**	**Comment**
Is brave	A	Josephine was willing to participate although she new little English.
Prepared to speak English		
Is creative		
Is confident		

Literary Report Card

Who was the main character of the story?

What was the setting of the story?

Why was Nasrettin's coat all dirty?

Why would no one talk to Nasrettin at his friend's party?

How did the story end?

What do you think is the moral of the story?

The Hungry Coat: A Tale from Turkey

Questions for Story Elements in The Hungry Coat

Special Celebrations!

1. What is one holiday/celebration your country celebrates?

_____

_____

_____

_____

2. What are some special traditions that are related to this holiday/celebration?

_____

_____

_____

_____

_____

_____

_____

_____

_____

_____

3. Do we have a holiday/celebration that is similar? If yes, please explain.

_____

_____

_____

_____

_____

_____

_____

_____

_____

Special Celebrations

Could it be True?

While discussing whether illustrations from the story are realistic or fantasy, record your thoughts below in the appropriate column. Compare your chart to the class chart and discuss findings.

<u>Realistic</u>   **<u>Fantasy</u>**

Could It Be True?

My Favorite

Students will design their own locket using construction paper and the attached pattern for "My Favorite Locket." They will cut out two patterns and glue the two sides together. Inside the locket on the left students will illustrate and write a sentence about their favorite event from the story. On the right side students will recall and write the title, author, characters, and setting of the story. Students will decorate the outside of the locket however they wish. When finished students will make the locket into a necklace using yarn. Students will wear and share their lockets with the class.

See attached patterns!

My Favorite Locket

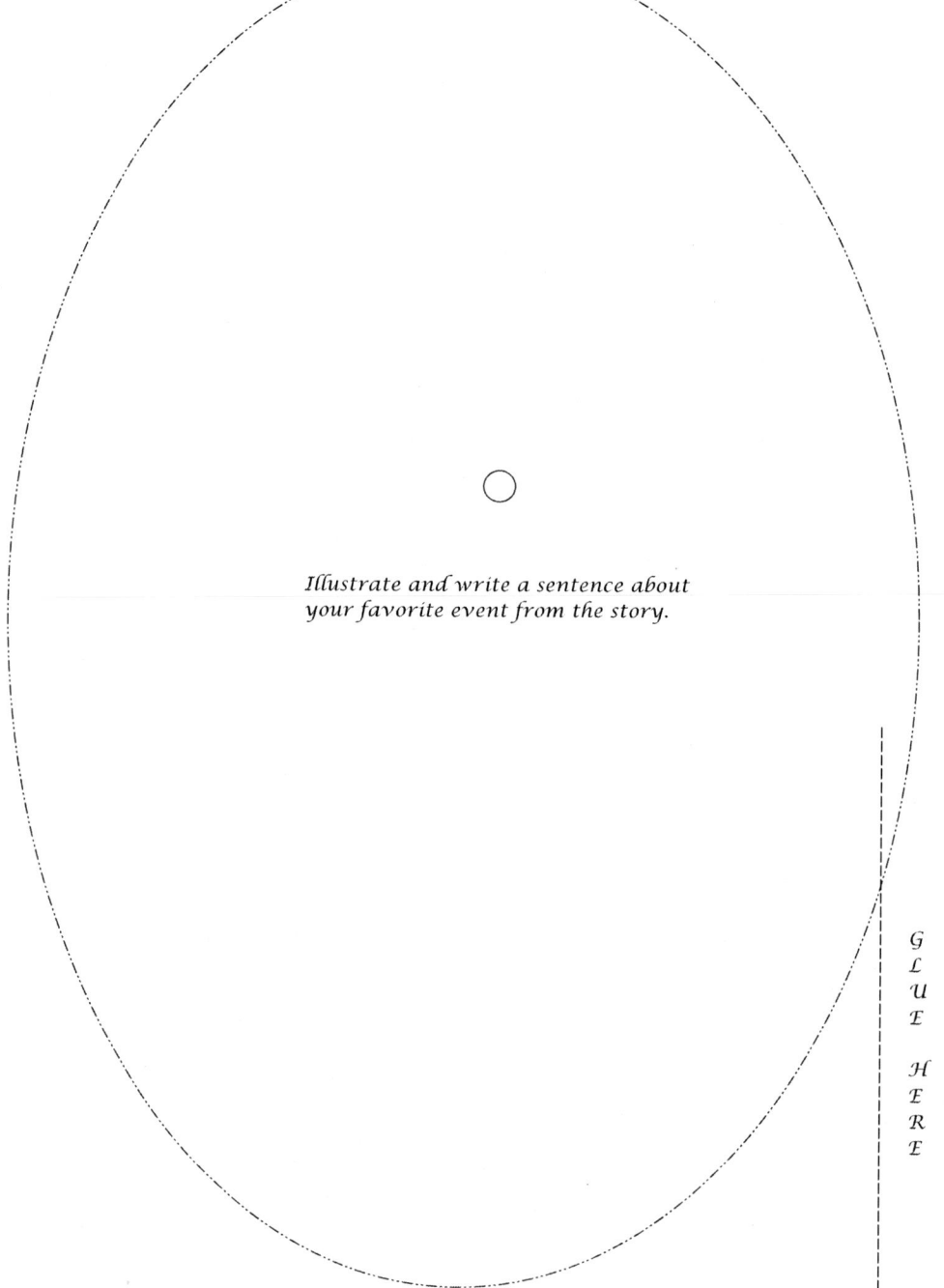

Illustrate and write a sentence about your favorite event from the story.

G
L
U
E

H
E
R
E

My Favorite Locket (continued)

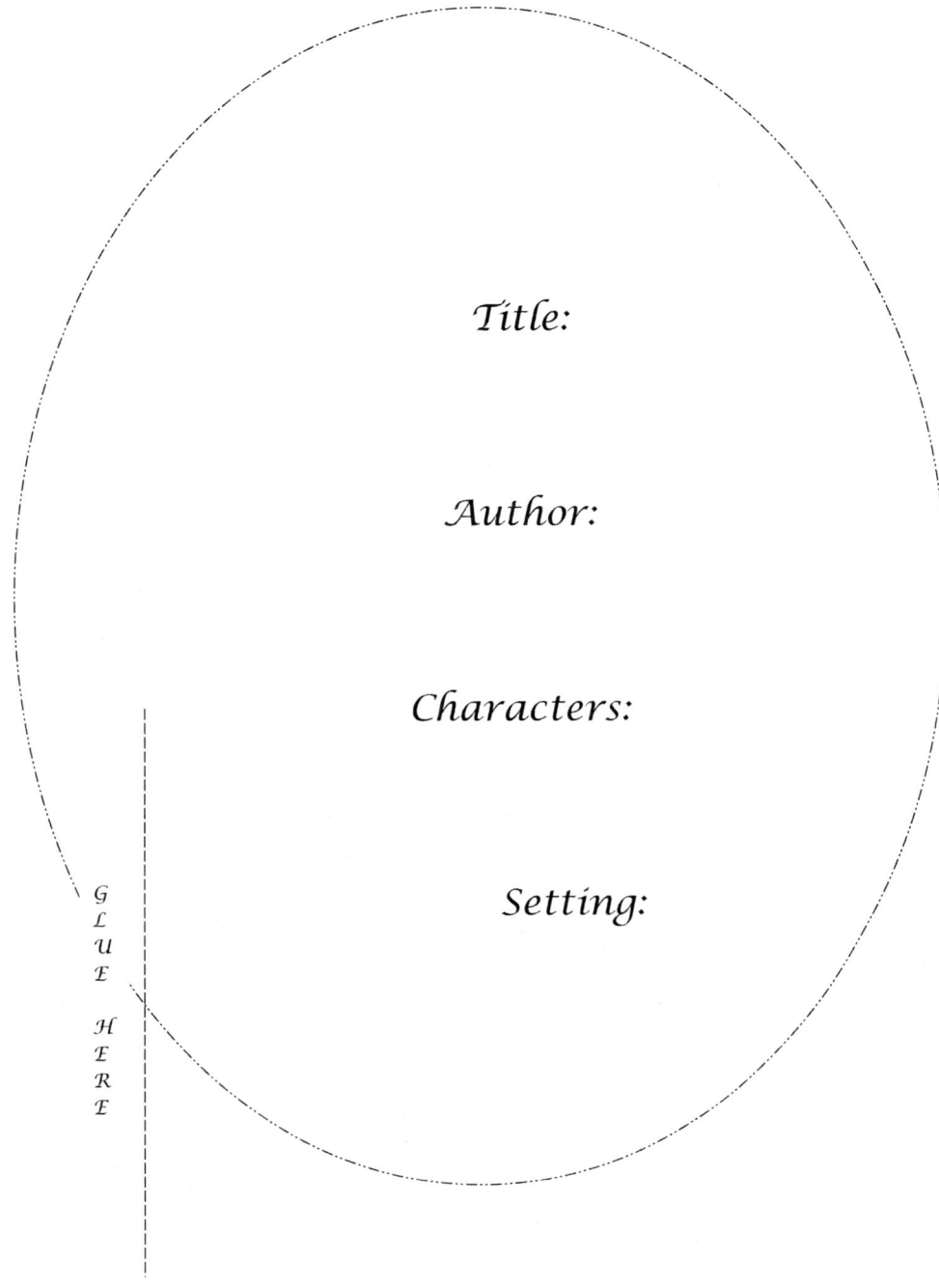

Title:

Author:

Characters:

Setting:

G
L
U
E

H
E
R
E

My Favorite Locket (continued)

I march because…

I march because…

A Sweet Smell of Roses

I March Because

Four Square Vocabulary

A Sweet Smell of Roses

Four Square Vocabulary

Double Entry Journal

Quote	Response

Double Entry Journal

My Family Invitation

Occasion_____

Place_____

Date_____

Time_____

Family

My Family Invitation

Because...

Am I a Color Too?

Because . . .

Paw Prints for The Good Luck Cat

Feelings Chart

Events	My Feelings

Feelings Chart

Book Review Team
Am I a Color Too?
By Heidi Cole and Nancy Vogl

The Good Luck Cat

Team Members_____

1. One thing we liked about this book was

_____

_____
_____

_____.
_____
----

because_____

_____.

2. One thing we liked least about this book was

_____

_____
_____

_____.
_____
----

because_____

_____.

3. On a scale of 1 – 10, we rate the book as: _____

Book Review I

Book Review Team
Am I a Color Too?
By Heidi Cole and Nancy Vogl

Team Members_____

   1. One thing we liked about this book was_____

        _____

        because_____

        _____.

   2. One thing we liked least about this book was_____

        _____

        because_____

        _____.

   3. Our favorite part was_____

        _____

        because_____

        _____.

   4. One thing we would change is _____

        _____

        because_____

        _____.

   5. We would recommend this book to_____.

   6. On a scale of 1 – 10, we rate the book as: _____

Am I a Color Too?

Book Review II

Sentence Sequence

The beautiful pot that Juan built.
That left manure all over the ground
That fueled the flames so sizzling hot
These are the cows all white and brown
That flickered and flared and fired the pot,

The Pot That Juan Built

Sentence Sequence I

Sentence Sequence

The crackling flames so sizzling hot
These are the rocks of red and black
That flickered and flared and fired the pot,
Brought down from the mountain on burro-back
That beautiful pot that Juan built.
To make into paint all black and red
Spread with the brush of hair from his head
Before it was baked in the cow manure fire,
That colored the pot for all to admire

Sentence Sequence II

Clarifying Words

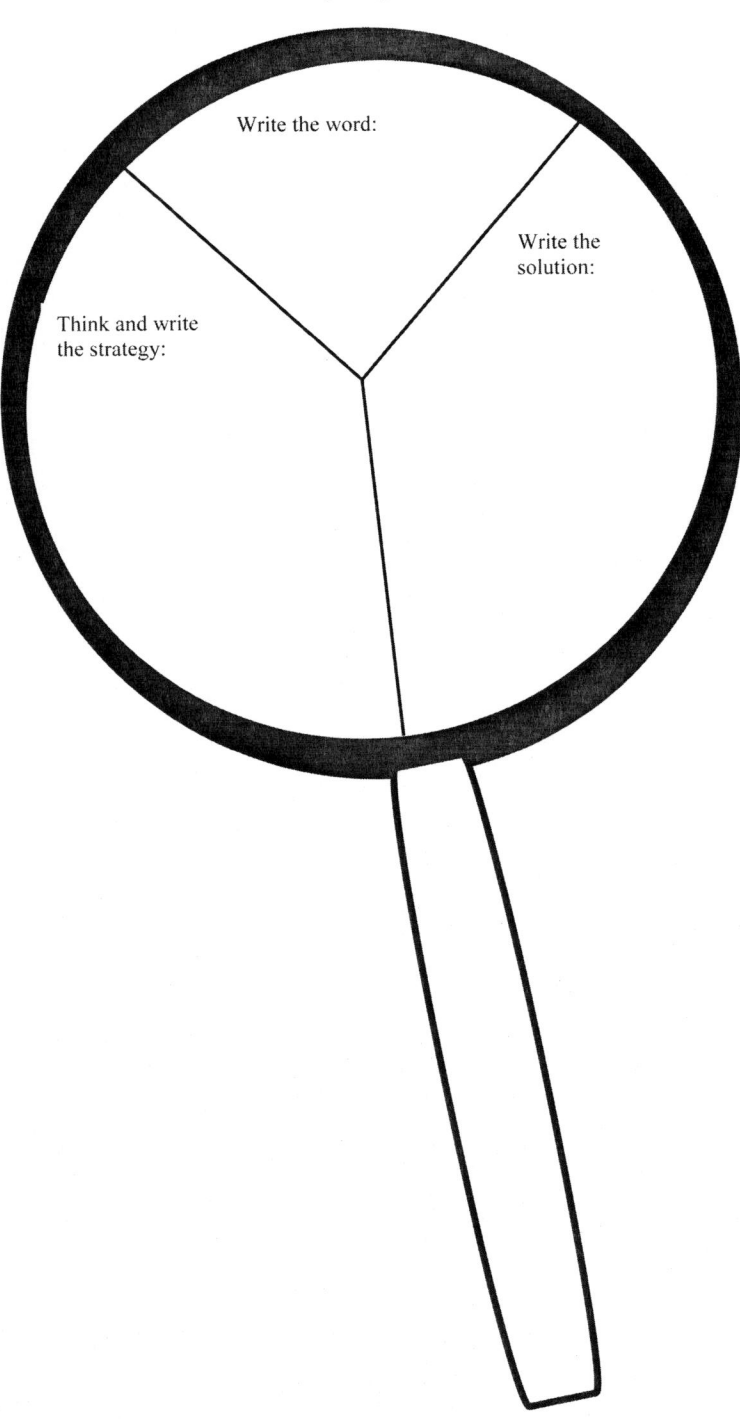

Clarifying Words

WORD SORT

Grandma	siete	ven
seven	**How are you?**	six
red	tres	**Feliz cumpleanos!**
five	orgullo	three
seis	yellow	**Abuelita**
Abuelito	one	proud
come	cinco	two
cuatro	**Grandpa**	como estas?
Happy Birthday	uno	four
Amarillo	rojo	dos

I love Saturdays y domingos

Word Sort

Title:
Author:

Discussion Web

<u>YES</u>   <u>NO</u>

Was it right for Clover and Annie to spend time together?

Conclusion:

The Other Side

Discussion Web

Compare and Contrast
Brazil vs United States

Topic:	Brazil	United States
The Land		
Language		
Transportation		
Cultural Families		
School		
Food		
Sports		

Brazil

Compare and Contrast (Brazil and United States)

Can You Imagine?

By: _____

Can you imagine _____

_____

Can you imagine _____

_____

Can you imagine _____

_____

Can you imagine _____

_____

Can you imagine _____

_____

Can you imagine _____

_____

Can you imagine _____

_____

My Name is Gabito

Can You Imagine?

Compare and Contrast

Me: _____   Tomasino

How are we alike?

_____

_____

_____

_____

_____

How are we different?

_____
_____
_____
_____

_____
_____
_____
_____

Tomasino: A Child of Peru

Compare and Contrast (Me and Tomasino)

Venezuela

Template for Class Book

Aa

Template for Class Book 1

Blank Cards for Alphabetizing Vocabulary Activity

Venezuela

Blank Cards for Alphabetizing Vocabulary Activity

APPENDIX B

Common Core State Standards Matrix (K–3)

Common Core State Standards: Kindergarten		Literacy Activities (Page Numbers)
Reading: Literature		
Key Ideas and Details	RL.K.1–RL.K.3	12, 16, 19, 22, 23, 30, 33, 34, 38, 40, 41, 42, 50, 51, 53, 56, 64, 67, 70, 72, 73, 80, 83, 85, 86, 88, 89, 90, 96, 99, 101, 109, 111, 113, 114, 116, 118, 120, 122, 123, 125, 126, 138, 139, 140, 141, 143, 145
Craft and Structure	RL.K.4–RL.K.6	35, 57, 83, 98, 115, 116, 124
Integration of Knowledge and Ideas	RL.K.7–RL.K.9	35, 39, 64, 67, 70, 81, 96, 101, 108, 110, 125, 138, 143
Range of Reading and Level of Text Complexity	RL.K.10	30
Reading: Informational Text		
Key Ideas and Details	RI.K.1–RI.K.3	41, 101
Craft and Structure	RI.K.4–RI.K.6	37, 144
Reading: Foundational Skills		
Fluency	RF.K.4	80, 118, 141, 147
Writing		
Text Types and Purposes	W.K.1–W.K.3	23, 37, 40, 42, 51, 53, 55, 56, 57, 69, 70, 73, 74, 87, 98, 100, 109, 112, 113, 116, 118, 120, 121, 122, 126, 139, 140, 141, 142, 144
Production and Distribution of Writing	W.K.5–W.K.6	30, 32, 57, 69, 100
Research to Build and Present Knowledge	W.K.7–W.K.8	22, 34, 85, 86, 123, 124, 139, 141, 147

Common Core State Standards Matrix (K–3) (*continued*)

Speaking and Listening		
Comprehension and Collaboration	SL.K.1–SL.K.3	12, 19, 73, 80, 85, 86, 90, 110, 111, 112, 113, 116, 118, 119, 123, 124, 139, 143
Presentation of Knowledge and Ideas	SL.K.4–SL.K.6	140
Language		
Conventions of Standard English	L.K.1–L.K.2	102
Vocabulary Acquisition and Use	L.K.4–L.K.6	30, 33, 39, 54, 102, 108, 111, 120, 126, 139, 144

Common Core State Standards: Grade 1		*Literacy Activities (Page Numbers)*
Reading: Literature		
Key Ideas and Details	RL.1.1–RL.1.3	12, 13, 16, 19, 22, 23, 30, 33, 34, 38, 40, 41, 42, 50, 51, 53, 56, 64, 67, 70, 72, 73, 80, 83, 85, 86, 88, 89, 90, 96, 99, 101, 109, 111, 113, 114, 116, 118, 120, 122, 123, 124, 125, 126, 138, 139, 140, 141, 143, 145
Craft and Structure	RL.1.4–RL.1.6	35, 57, 83, 98, 115, 116, 124
Integration of Knowledge and Ideas	RL.1.7–RL.1.9	24, 35, 39, 64, 66, 67, 70, 81, 96, 101, 108, 110, 123, 125, 138, 143
Range of Reading and Level of Text Complexity	RL.1.10	30, 114, 115
Reading: Informational Text		
Key Ideas and Details	RI.1.1–RI.1.3	41, 101
Craft and Structure	RI.1.4–RI.1.6	37, 67, 114
Reading: Foundational Skills		
Fluency	RF.1.4	80, 118, 141, 147

(*continued*)

Common Core State Standards Matrix (K–3) (*continued*)

Writing		
Text Types and Purposes	W.1.1 –W.1.3	19, 21, 23, 37, 40, 42, 51, 53, 55, 56, 57, 69, 70, 73, 74, 98, 100, 108, 112, 113, 116, 118, 119, 120, 121, 122, 126, 140, 141, 142, 144
Production and Distribution of Writing	W.1.5–W.1.6	30, 32, 57, 69, 100
Research to Build and Present Knowledge	W.1.7–W.1.8	22, 24, 34, 66, 85, 86, 88, 102, 123, 124, 139, 141, 145, 147
Speaking and Listening		
Comprehension and Collaboration	SL.1.1–SL.1.3	73, 80, 85, 86, 90, 108, 110, 111, 112, 113, 116, 118, 119, 123, 124, 139, 143
Presentation of Knowledge and Ideas	SL.1.4–SL.1.6	82, 140
Language		
Conventions of Standard English	L.1.1–L.1.2	102, 121
Vocabulary Acquisition and Use	L.1.4–L.1.6	20, 30, 33, 39, 64, 96, 102, 108, 111, 120, 126, 139, 144, 147

Common Core State Standards: Grade 2		*Literacy Activities (Page Numbers)*
Reading: Literature		
Key Ideas and Details	RL.2.1–RL.2.3	12, 13, 16, 19, 22, 23, 30, 33, 34, 38, 40, 41, 42, 48, 49, 50, 51, 53, 56, 64, 67, 70, 72, 73, 80, 83, 85, 86, 88, 89, 90, 96, 99, 101, 109, 111, 113, 114, 116, 118, 120, 122, 123, 124, 125, 126, 138, 139, 140, 141, 143, 145
Craft and Structure	RL.2.4–RL.2.6	35, 41, 48, 57, 67, 83, 98, 115, 116, 124
Integration of Knowledge and Ideas	RL.2.7–RL.2.9	24, 35, 39, 64, 66, 67, 70, 81, 101, 108, 110, 125, 138, 143
Range of Reading and Level of Text Complexity	RL.2.10	30, 114, 115

Common Core State Standards Matrix (K–3) (*continued*)

Reading: Informational Text		
Key Ideas and Details	RI.2.1–RI.2.3	101
Craft and Structure	RI.2.4–RI.2.6	37, 99, 144
Reading: Foundational Skills		
Fluency	RF.2.4	80, 118, 141, 147
Writing		
Text Types and Purposes	W.2.1 –W.2.3	14, 17, 19, 21, 23, 37, 40, 42, 51, 52, 53, 55, 56, 57, 69, 70, 73, 74, 98, 100, 108, 109, 112, 113, 116, 118, 119, 120, 121, 122, 126, 139, 140, 141, 142, 144
Production and Distribution of Writing	W.2.5–W.2.6	30, 32, 57, 69, 90, 100
Research to Build and Present Knowledge	W.2.7–W.2.8	22, 24, 34, 66, 85, 86, 88, 123, 124, 139, 141, 145, 147
Speaking and Listening		
Comprehension and Collaboration	SL.2.1–SL.2.3	73, 80, 85, 86, 90, 108, 110, 111, 112, 113, 116, 118, 119, 123, 124, 139
Presentation of Knowledge and Ideas	SL.2.4–SL.2.6	15, 17, 18, 21, 24, 32, 34, 37, 40, 43, 49, 52, 55, 58, 66, 69, 72, 75, 82, 85, 88, 90, 98, 100, 102, 110, 123, 124, 126, 140, 142, 143, 144, 147
Language		
Conventions of Standard English	L.2.1–L.2.2	100, 102, 121, 142
Knowledge of Language	L.2.3	139
Vocabulary Acquisition and Use	L.2.4–L.2.6	14, 16, 20, 30, 33, 36, 39, 48, 51, 54, 84, 96, 102, 108, 111, 112, 115, 117, 119, 120, 122, 139, 144, 147

(*continued*)

Common Core State Standards Matrix (K–3) (continued)

Common Core State Standards: Grade 3		Literacy Activities (Page Numbers)
Reading: Literature		
Key Ideas and Details	RL.3.1–RL.3.3	12, 13, 16, 19, 22, 23, 30, 33, 34, 38, 40, 41, 42, 48, 49, 50, 51, 53, 56, 64, 67, 70, 72, 73, 80, 83, 85, 86, 88, 89, 90, 96, 99, 101, 109, 111, 113, 114, 116, 118, 120, 122, 123, 124, 125, 126, 139, 140, 141, 143, 145
Craft and Structure	RL.3.4–RL.3.6	35, 41, 48, 57, 67, 83, 98, 115, 116, 124
Integration of Knowledge and Ideas	RL.3.7, RL.3.9	24, 35, 39, 64, 66, 67, 70, 81, 96, 101, 108, 110, 125, 138, 143
Range of Reading and Level of Text Complexity	RL.3.10	30, 114, 115
Reading: Informational Text		
Key Ideas and Details	RI.3.1–RI.3.3	101
Craft and Structure	RI.3.4–RI.3.6	37, 99, 144
Reading: Foundational Skills		
Fluency	RF.3.4	80, 118, 141, 147
Writing		
Text Types and Purposes	W.3.1 –W.3.3	14, 17, 19, 21, 23, 37, 40, 42, 51, 52, 53, 55, 56, 57, 69, 70, 73, 74, 98, 100, 108, 109, 112, 113, 116, 119, 120, 121, 122, 126, 139, 140, 141, 142
Production and Distribution of Writing	W.3.4–W.3.6	30, 32, 57, 69, 90, 100, 145
Research to Build and Present Knowledge	W.3.7–W.3.8	22, 24, 34, 66, 85, 86, 88, 123, 124, 139, 141, 145, 147
Speaking and Listening		
Comprehension and Collaboration	SL.3.1–SL.3.3	73, 80, 85, 86, 90, 108, 110, 111, 112, 113, 116, 119, 123, 124, 139

Common Core State Standards Matrix (K–3) (*continued*)

Presentation of Knowledge and Ideas	SL.3.4–SL.3.6	15, 17, 18, 21, 24, 32, 34, 37, 40, 43, 49, 52, 55, 58, 66, 69, 72, 75, 82, 85, 88, 90, 98, 100, 102, 110, 123, 124, 126, 140, 142, 143, 144, 147
Language		
Conventions of Standard English	L.3.1–L.3.2	100, 102, 121, 142
Knowledge of Language	L.3.3	139
Vocabulary Acquisition and Use	L.3.4–L.3.6	14, 16, 20, 30, 33, 39, 48, 54, 84, 96, 102, 108, 111, 112, 115, 117, 119, 120, 122, 139, 144, 147

Podcast Resources

Podcasts (document, websites, tutorials, etc.)	Description
Making a Podcast https://www.apple.com/itunes/podcasts/specs.html	iTunes- and Mac-based complete overview of creating podcasts, uploading them, tracking their usage, etc.
How to Start Your Own Podcast http://www.wikihow.com/Start-Your-Own-Podcast	PC-based, a wiki that provides four steps to create a podcast: before the podcast, creating the podcast, uploading the podcast, and making money from the podcast. This site also includes a video on how to create a podcast.
How to Create Your Own Podcast: A Step-by-Step Tutorial http://radio.about.com/od/createyourownpodcast/ss/How-to-Create-Your-Own-Podcast-Make-Your-Own-Talk-Show-Music-Program-or-Audio-Stream.htm	This article shows the differences between podcasting and Internet radio. It also shows different websites to create a podcast on. A portion goes on to explain why you should create a podcast.
How to Create a Successful Podcast: Just Say Yes! http://www.theguardian.com/lifeandstyle/2014/nov/11/how-to-create-a-successful-podcast-just-say-yes	This article shows the insights of a very successful podcaster, Helen Zaltzman, and she gives tips on how to create and become big in the world of podcasting. She is mainly PC-based.
What Is a Podcast and How Do I Create One? http://etc.usf.edu/techease/mac/internet/what-is-a-podcast-and-how-do-i-create-one/	This resource mainly focuses on Mac-based podcasting. It first goes into short explanations of how to create a podcast and then provides videos about each step.
Start Your Own Podcast http://www.macworld.com/article/1044428/junecreate.html	An article designed for Mac users to create a podcast. This article details the equipment necessary, how to record, edit, and upload your podcast. Finally, it explains how to promote your podcast.

Podcast Rubrics

Kathy Schrock's Guide to Everything http://www.schrockguide.net/assessment-and -rubrics.html	This resource contains a plethora of assessments and rubrics. Schrock provides five podcast rubrics for different purposes: one for educators and the rest for the students. Her rubrics are made for middle school students.
Fossum Middle School: 2013–2014 http://mcallenisd.fossum.schoolfusion.us/modules/ cms/pages.phtml?sessionid=&pageid=232212	This school provides a short list (five) of podcast rubrics for students and educators to use.
What Is a Podcast? http://webtools4u2use.wikispaces.com/ Audio+%26+Podcasting	This site contains instructions on how to create podcasts and about eighteen different rubrics for creating and grading them.
Assessing Student Learning http://edtechteacher.org/assessment/	This website is a large database of assessments for educators to use. The podcast rubrics are a small part of the website, but it has about seven resources about grading and using podcasts.
How to Podcast http://www.how-to-podcast-tutorial.com/ podcasting-articles.htm	This website provides a step-by-step guide for creating podcasts.

Additional Digital Sources

Digital Storytelling http://www.storycenter.org/	Resources for creating digital stories.
Digistory http://www.digistory.org	Resources and examples of digital storytelling in education.
Little Bird Tales http://littlebirdtales.com/	Resource for creating children's eBooks with original artwork and their voices!
iBooks Author http://www.apple.com/ibooks-author/	Multimedia/interactive book editor.

Name	Description	Audience	Web address
ePals	ePals enriches K-12 learning in the classroom and at home with innovative web-based tools and the highest standard of children's stories, games and digital media on the Web.	all grade levels	http://www.e pals.com/#!/ main
African Studies Center - Bibliography of Children's Literature	The books on this list are stories with children as the main characters. They are meant to give accurate portrayals of life in the country in which the story takes place. There are a variety of social and cultural situations. The books listed are just titles and educators would need to get the actual books from a different source. The books listed here are mainly of African heritage and culture.	all grade levels	http://www.b u.edu/africa/ outreach/res ources/childb ib/
Literature for Young People - Islamic Traditions and Muslim Cultures	This page gives a long list of young people's literature items. This list focuses mainly on Islamic Traditions and Muslim Cultures.	all grade levels	http://commi nfo.rutgers.e du/professio nal-develop ment/childlit/ ChildrenLit/is lamicliterature.htm
The School Library Journal - Resources for Finding Latino Kid Lit	This article provides a great hub for educators looking for Latino based children's literature sites. It includes: book lists, websites, publishers that specialize in Latino Kids Lit, popular and award winning latino authors and illustrators, and professional development items.	all grade levels	http://www.slj .com/2013/0 1/collection-d evelopment/r esources-for- finding-latino -kid-lit/
San Francisco Public Library - Kids	This website has three pages devoted to multicultural children's books - Asian, Latino, and Middle Eastern. Each listing gives the title of the book, the author, a short blurb, and the age group it is best suited for. Some even have a list of related book to each book listed.	educators & early childhood grade levels	http://sfpl.org /index.php?p g=20001541 01

REFERENCES

Abadiano, H., and J. Turner. (2007). "New Literacies, New Challenges." *The New England Reading Association Journal* 43(1): 75–78.

Allen, J. (1999). *Words, Words, Words.* Portsmouth, NH: Heinemann.

Allen, J. (2004). *Tools for Teaching Content Literacy.* Portland, ME: Stenhouse Publishers.

Alvermann, D.E. (1991). "The Discussion Web: A graphic aid for learning across the curriculum." *The Reading Teacher*, 45, 92-99.

Anderson, R. C., and P. D. Pearson. (1984). "A Schema-Thematic View of Basic Processes in Reading Comprehension." In P. D. Pearson, R. Barr, M. L. Kamil, and P. Mosenthal, eds. *Handbook of Reading Research* (pp. 255–91). New York: Longman.

Banks, J. (2006). *Race, Culture, and Education: The Selected Works of James A Banks.* New York: Routledge.

Bear, D. R., M. Invernizzi, S. Templeton, and F. Johnston. (2004). *Words Their Way: Word Study for Phonics, Vocabulary, and Spelling Instruction* (3rd ed.). Upper Saddle River, NJ: Merrill/Prentice Hall.

Boxie, P. (2004). "Cybermentoring: An Online Literacy Project in Teacher Education." *Technological Horizons in Education Journal* 32(2): 32–37.

Boxie, P., and G. H. Maring. (2001). *Cybermentoring: The Relationship between Preservice Teachers' Use of Online Literacy Strategies and Student Achievement.* Reading Online.

Bromley, K.D. (1996). *Webbing with Literature: Creating Story Maps with Children's Books* (2nd ed). Needham Heights, MA: Allyn and Bacon.

Carr, E., and D. M. Ogle. (1987). "K_W_L_Plus: A Strategy for Comprehension and Summarization." *Journal of Reading* 30: 626–31.

Common Core State Standards. (2010). *Common Core State Standards for English Language Arts & Literacy in History/Social Studies, Science and Technical Subjects.* Retrieved from http://www.corestandards.org/thestandards.

Davey, B. (1983). "Think Aloud: Modeling the Cognitive Processes for Reading Comprehension." *Journal of Reading,* 27 (1), 44-47.

Duffy, G., L. Roehler, and B. A. Herrmann. (1998). "Modeling Mental Process Helps Poor Readers Become Strategic Readers." In R. Allington, ed., *Teaching Struggling Readers: Articles from the Reading Teacher* (pp. 162–67). Newark, DE: International Reading Association.

Fountas, I. C., and G. S. Pinnell. (2001). *Guiding Readers and Writers Grades 3–6: Teaching Comprehension, Genre, and Content Literacy.* Portsmouth, NH: Heinemann.

Frayer, D., W. C. Frederick, and H. J. Klausmeier. (1969). *A Schema for Testing the Level of Cognitive Mastery.* Madison: Wisconsin Center for Education Research.

Gooch, K., and P. Saine. (2011). "Integration of the Visual Arts and Web 2.0 Technologies in the Classroom." *New England Reading Association Journal (NERAJ)* 47(1): 92–100.

Haberman, M. (1993). "Predicting the Success of Urban Teachers (The Milwaukee Trials)." *Action in Teacher Education* 15(3): 1–5.

Hadaway, N. L., and M. J. McKenna. (2007). *Breaking Boundaries with Global Literature: Celebrating Diversity in K–12 Classrooms.* Portsmouth, NH: International Reading Association.

Harris, V. J. (1997). *Using Multiethnic Literature in the K–8 Classroom.* Norwood, MA: Christopher Gordon.

Harste, J., K. Short, and C. Burke. (1988). *Creating Classrooms for Authors: The Reading-Writing Connections.* Portsmouth, NH: Heinemann.

Harste, J., V. Woodward, and C. Burke. (1984). *Language Stories and Literacy Lessons.* Portsmouth, NH: Heinemann.

Hoyt, L. (1999). *Revisit, Reflect, Retell.* Portsmouth, NH: Heinemann.

Johnson, T.D., and Louis, D.R. (1987). *Bringing It All Together: A Program for Literacy.* North Ryde, N.SW: Methuen.

Karchmer, R. A., D. J. Leu, M. H. Mallette, and J. Kara-Soteriou, eds. (2005). *New Literacies for New Times: Innovative Models of Literacy Education Using the Internet.* Newark, DE: International Reading Association.

Karchmer-Klein, R., V. H. Shinas, and S. Park. (2014). "Framing K–12 Multimodal Digital Writing Instruction." In R. Anderson and C. Mims, eds., *Digital Tools for Writing Instruction in K–12 Settings: Student Perception and Experience* (pp. 499–519). Hershey, PA: IGI Global.

Ladson-Billing, G. (1999). "Preparing Teachers for Diverse Student Population: A Critical Race Theory Perspective." In A. Iran-Nejad and D. Pearson, eds., *Review of Research in Education* (Vol. 24, pp. 221–48). Washington, DC: American Educational Research Association.

Lee, C. D. (2005). "Intervention Research Based on Current Cognitive Views of Learning." In Joyce E. King, ed., *Black Education: A Transformative Research and*

Action Agenda for the New Century (pp. 73–114). Mahwah, NJ: Lawrence Erlbaum Associates.

Leu, D. J., and C. K. Kinzer. (2000). "The Convergence of Literacy Instruction with Networked Technologies for Information and Communication." *Reading Research Quarterly* 35(1): 108–27.

Leu, D. J., Jr., C. K. Kinzer, J. Coiro, and D. Cammack. (2004). *Toward a Theory of New Literacies Emerging from the Internet and Other Information and Communication Technologies.* Readingonline.org.

Macon, J.M., Bewell, D., Vogt, M.E., and International Reading Association. (1991). *Responses to Literature.* Newark, DE: International Reading Association.

McKenna, M. J. (2007). "Crossing the Bridge." In N. Hadaway and M. McKenna, eds., *Breaking Boundaries with Global Literature: Celebrating Diversity in K–12 Classrooms* (p. l83). Portsmouth, NH: International Reading Association.

Miller, D. (2002). *Reading with Meaning: Teaching Comprehension in the Primary Grades.* Portland, ME: Stenhouse Publishers.

Nagy, W. E. (1988). *Teaching Vocabulary to Improve Reading Comprehension.* Urbana, IL: ERIC Clearinghouse on Reading and Communication Skills and the National Council of Teachers of English and the International Reading Association.

Oczkus, L. (2003). *Reciprocal Teaching at Work: Strategies for Improving Reading Comprehension.* Newark, DE: International Reading Association.

Ogle, D. (1986). "KWL: A Teaching Model That Develops Active Reading of Expository Text." *Reading Teacher* 39: 563–70.

Pang, V. O. (2001). *Multicultural Education: A Caring Centered Reflective Approach.* New York: McGraw-Hill Higher Education.

Piaget, J. (1963). *Origins of Intelligence in Children.* New York: Norton.

Pressley, M. (1995). *Cognitive Strategy Instruction That Really Improves Children's Academic Performance.* Cambridge, MA: Brookline Books.

Rasinski, T. (2003). *The Fluent Reader.* New York: Scholastic.

Readance, J., T. Bean, and R. Baldwin. (1989). *Content Area Reading: An Integrated Approach.* Dubuque, IA: Kendall/Hunt.

Rosenblatt, L. (1978). *The Reader, the Text, the Poem: The Transactional Theory of the Literary Work.* Carbondale, IL: Southern Illinois University Press.

Saine, P., and J. Kara-Soteriou. (2010). "Using Podcasts to Enrich Responses to Global Children's Literature." *New England Reading Association Journal (NERAJ)* 46(1): 100–108.

Schultz, E., T. Nehart, and U. Reck. (1996). "Swimming against the Tide: A Study of Prospective Teachers' Attitudes Regarding Cultural Diversity and Urban Teaching." *Western Journal of Black Studies* 20(1): 1–7.

Sims-Bishop, R. (1990). "Mirrors, Windows, and Sliding Glass Doors." *Perspectives* 6: ix–xi.

Stahl, S. A. (1999). *Vocabulary Development.* Cambridge, MA: Brookline Books.

Stahl, S.A. (2004).*Vocabulary learning and the child with learning disabilities.* Perspectives, 30, 1. The International Dyslexia Association.

Stauffer, R. (1980). *The Language Experience Approach to the Teaching of Reading* (2nd ed.). New York: Harper & Row.

Stephens, E. C., and J. E. Brown. (2000). *A Handbook of Content Literacy Strategies: 75 Practical Reading and Writing Ideas.* Norwood, MA: Christopher Gordon.

Terill, M., and D. L. H. Mark. (2000). "Preservice Teachers' Expectations for Schools with Children of Color and Second-Language Learners." *Journal of Teacher Education* 51(2): 149–55.

Tyner, K. (1998). *Literacy in a Digital World: Teaching and Learning in the Age of Information.* Mahwah, NJ: Lawrence Erlbaum Associates.

Vygotsky, L. S. (1978). *Mind in Society: The Development of Higher Psychological Processes.* Edited by M. Cole, V. John-Steiner, S. Scribner, and E. Sourberman. Cambridge, MA: Harvard University Press.

Wilhelm, J. (2001). *Improving Comprehension with Think-Aloud Strategies: Modeling What Good Readers Do.* New York: Scholastic Professional.

Yopp, R. H., and H. K. Yopp. (2002). "Ten Important Words: Identifying the Big Ideas in Informational Text." *Journal of Content Area Reading* 2: 7–13.

CHILDREN'S LITERATURE REFERENCES

Ada Flor, Alma. (2002). *I Love Saturdays y Domingos.* New York: Simon & Schuster Children's Publishing Division.

Andrews-Goebel, Nancy. (2002). *The Pot That Juan Built.* New York: Lee & Low Books Inc.

Arugueta, Jorge. (2007). *Alfredito Flies Home.* Toronto, ON: Groundwod Books.

Bercaw, Edna. (2000). *Halmoni's Day.* New York: Dial Books for Young Readers.

Bootman, Colin. (2006). *Fish for the Grand Lady.* New York: Holiday House.

Brown, Monica. (2007). *My Name Is Gabito.* Flagstaff, AZ: Luna Rising.

Bulion, Leslie. (2002). *Fatuma's New Cloth.* North Kingstown, RI: Moon Mountain Publishing.

Cole, Heidi, and Nancy Vogl. (2005). *Am I a Color Too?* Bellevue, WA: Illumination Arts.

Cooper, Floyd. (1996). *Mandela: From the Life of a South Africa Statesman.* New York: Penguin Putnam Books.

Cooper, Sharon Kutz. (2007). *Venezuela ABCs.* Minneapolis, MN: Picture Windows Book.

Demi. (2004). *The Hungry Coat: A Tale from Turkey.* New York: Margaret K. McElderry Books.

Fleming, Candace. (2003). *Boxes for Katje.* New York: Farrar, Straus and Giroux.

Gelman, Rita. (2000). *Rice Is Life.* New York: Henry Holt & Company.

Gershator, Phillis. (2005). *Rata-Pata-Scata-Fata: A Caribbean Story.* New York: Star Bright Books, Inc.

Giraud, Herve. (2005). *Tomasino: A Child of Peru.* Detroit, MI: Blackbirch Press.

Grant, Karima. (2006). *Sofie and the City.* Honesdale, PA: Boyds Mill Press.

Gunning, Monica. (1998). *Under the Breadfruit Tree*. Honesdale, PA: Boyds Mills Press, Inc.

Harjo, Joy. (2000). *The Good Luck Cat*. San Diego, CA: Harcourt Inc.

Hash, Bill W. (2014). *Jahmon's Adventure Home*. Mustang, OK: Tate Publishing and Enterprises.

Howard, Ginger. (2002). *Basket of Bangles: How a Business Begins*. Brookfield, CT: Millbrook Press, Inc.

Ichikawa, Satomi. (2006). *My Father's Shop*. LaJolla, CA: Kane/Miller Publications.

Johnson, Angela. (2005). *A Sweet Smell of Roses*. New York: Simon & Schuster Books for Young Readers.

Krishnawami, Umd. (2003). *Monsoon*. New York: Farrar, Straus and Giroux.

Kyuchukov, Hristo. (2004). *My Name Was Hussein*. Honesdale, PA: Boyds Mill Press.

Mak, Kim. (2002). *My Chinatown: One Year in Poems*. New York, NY: Harper Collins Publishers.

Monk, Isabell. (2001). *Family*. Minneapolis, MN: Scholastic, Inc.

Nobisso, Josephine. (2002). *In English, Of Course*. New York: Gingerbread House.

Russell, Barbara Timberlake. (2004). *The Remembering Stone*. New York: Farrar, Straus and Giroux.

Say, Allen. (2005). *Kamishibai Man*. New York: Houghton Mifflin Company.

Smith, Cynthia. (2000). *Jingle Dancer*. New York: Morrow Junior Books.

Uegaki, Chieru. (2003). *Suki's Kimono*. Tonawanda, NY: Kids Can Press.

Weitzman, Elizabeth (2008). *Brazil*. Minneapolis, MN: Lerner Publishing Group.

Williams, Karen. (2005). *Circles of Hope*. Grand Rapids, MI: Eerdmans Books for Young Readers.

Williams, Karen Lynn. (2007). *Four Feet, Two Sandals*. Grand Rapids, MI: Eerdmans Books for Young Readers.

Woodson, Jacqueline. (2001). *The Other Side*. New York: G. P. Putnam's Sons.

Yee, Paul. (2004). *A Song for Ba*. Toronto, ON: Groundwood Books Douglas & McIntyre.

OTHER SOURCES

Baker, C. P. (2004). *Moon Costa Rica*. 5th ed. Emeryville: Avalon Travel Publishing.

Central Intelligence Agency. (2014). "Afghanistan." *The World Factbook*. Retrieved May 15, 2014, from https://www.cia.gov/library/publications/the-world-factbook/geos/af.html.

Central Intelligence Agency. (2014). "Bangladesh." *The World Factbook*. Retrieved May 10, 2014, from https://www.cia.gov/library/publications/the-world-factbook/geos/bg.html.

Central Intelligence Agency. (2014). "Belize." *The World Factbook*. Retrieved May 13, 2014, from https://www.cia.gov/library/publications/the-world-factbook/geos/bh.html.

Central Intelligence Agency. (2014). "Bulgaria." *The World Factbook*. Retrieved May 19, 2014, from https://www.cia.gov/library/publications/the-world-factbook/geos/bu.html.

Central Intelligence Agency. (2014). "China." *The World Factbook*. Retrieved April 24, 2014, from https://www.cia.gov/library/publications/the-world-factbook/geos/ch.html.

Central Intelligence Agency. (2014). "El Salvador." *The World Factbook*. Retrieved May 14, 2014, from https://www.cia.gov/library/publications/the-world-factbook/geos/es.html.

Central Intelligence Agency. (2014). "Haiti." *The World Factbook*. Retrieved May 11, 2014, from https://www.cia.gov/library/publications/the-world-factbook/geos/ha.html.

Central Intelligence Agency. (2014). "India." *The World Factbook*. Retrieved May 10, 2014, from https://www.cia.gov/library/publications/the-world-factbook/geos/in.html.

Central Intelligence Agency. (2014). "Indonesia." *The World Factbook*. Retrieved May 11, 2014, from https://www.cia.gov/library/publications/the-world-factbook/geos/id.html.

Central Intelligence Agency. (2014). "Italy." *The World Factbook*. Retrieved May 20, 2014, from https://www.cia.gov/library/publications/the-world-factbook/geos/it.html.

Central Intelligence Agency. (2014). "Jamaica." *The World Factbook*. Retrieved May 12, 2014, from https://www.cia.gov/library/publications/the-world-factbook/geos/jm.html.

Central Intelligence Agency (2014). "Japan." *The World Factbook*. Retrieved April 28, 2014, from https://www.cia.gov/library/publications/the-world-factbook/geos/ja.html.

Central Intelligence Agency. (2014). "Kenya." *The World Factbook*. Retrieved April 14, 2014, from https://www.cia.gov/library/publications/the-world-factbook/geos/ke.html.

Central Intelligence Agency. (2014). "Morocco." *The World Factbook*. Retrieved April 14, 2014, from https://www.cia.gov/library/publications/the-world-factbook/geos/mo.html.

Central Intelligence Agency. (2014). "North Korea." *The World Factbook*. Retrieved May 11, 2014, from https://www.cia.gov/library/publications/the-world-factbook/geos/kn.html.

Central Intelligence Agency. (2014). "Senegal." *The World Factbook*. Retrieved April 14, 2014, from https://www.cia.gov/library/publications/the-world-factbook/geos/sg.html.

Central Intelligence Agency. (2014). "South Africa." *The World Factbook*. Retrieved April 21, 2014, from https://www.cia.gov/library/publications/the-world-factbook/geos/sf.html.

Central Intelligence Agency. (2014). "South Korea." *The World Factbook*. Retrieved April 29, 2014, from https://www.cia.gov/library/publications/the-world-factbook/geos/ks.html.

Central Intelligence Agency. (2014). "St. Thomas." *The World Factbook*. Retrieved May 12, 2014, from https://www.cia.gov/library/publications/the-world-factbook/geos/vq.html.

Central Intelligence Agency. (2014). "Trinidad and Tobago." *The World Factbook*. Retrieved May 12, 2014, from https://www.cia.gov/library/publications/the-world-factbook/geos/td.html.

Central Intelligence Agency. (2014). "Turkey." *The World Factbook*. Retrieved May 17, 2014, from https://www.cia.gov/library/publications/the-world-factbook/geos/tu.html.

Communism. (2014). *Encyclopædia Britannica.* Retrieved April 24, 2014, from Encyclopedia Britannica Online, http://www.britannica.com/eb/article-9117284.

Country Studies: Bulgaria. (2014). The Library of Congress. http://lcweb2.loc.gov/frd/cs/bgtoc.html.

European Countries: Italy. (2014). *Europa.* Retrieved May 20, 2014, from http://europa.eu/abc/european_countries/eu_members/italy/index_en.htm.

Friedman, Barbara G., and John D. Richardson. (2014). "A National Disgrace." *Journalism History* 33(4): 224–232. Retrieved May 20, 2014, from EBSCO database.

Japan Fact Sheet. (2014). Web Japan. Retrieved April 28, 2014, from http://web-japan.org/factsheet.

Richie, D., and J. L. Anderson. (1958). "Traditional Theater and the Film in Japan." *Film Quarterly* 12(1): 2–9. Retrieved April 28, 2014, from JSTOR database.

Sweeney, A. (1979). "Rakugo Professional Japanese Storytelling." *Asian Folklore Studies* 38(1): 25–80. Retrieved April 28, 2014, from JSTOR database.

Turkish Culture. (2014). Turkish Cultural Foundation Official Web Site. Retrieved May 17, 2014, from http://www.turkishculture.org.

U.S. Department of State. (2014). "Background Note: Afghanistan." *Bureau of Public Affairs.* Retrieved May 15, 2014, from http://www.state.gov/r/pa/ei/bgn/5380.htm.

U.S. Department of State. (2014). "Background Note: Bangladesh." *Bureau of Public Affairs.* Retrieved May 10, 2014, from http://www.state.gov/r/pa/ei/bgn/3452.htm.

U.S. Department of State. (2014). "Background Note: Belize." *Bureau of Public Affairs.* Retrieved May 13, 2014, from http://www.state.gov/r/pa/ei/bgn/1955.htm.

U.S. Department of State. (2014). "Background Note: Bulgaria." *Bureau of Public Affairs.* Retrieved May 19, 2014, from http://www.state.gov/r/pa/ei/bgn/3236.htm.

U.S. Department of State. (2014). "Background Note: China." *Bureau of Public Affairs.* Retrieved April 24, 2014, from http://www.state.gov/r/pa/ei/bgn/18902.htm.

U.S. Department of State. (2014). "Background Note: El Salvador." *Bureau of Public Affairs.* Retrieved May 14, 2014, from http://www.state.gov/r/pa/ei/bgn/2033.htm.

U.S. Department of State. (2014). "Background Note: Haiti." *Bureau of Public Affairs.* Retrieved May 11, 2014, from http://www.state.gov/r/pa/ei/bgn/1982.htm.

U.S. Department of State. (2014). "Background Note: India." *Bureau of Public Affairs.* Retrieved May 10, 2014, from http://www.state.gov/r/pa/ei/bgn/3454.htm.

U.S. Department of State. (2014). "Background Note: Indonesia." *Bureau of Public Affairs.* Retrieved May 11, 2014, from http://www.state.gov/r/pa/ei/bgn/3452.htm.

U.S. Department of State. (2014). "Background Note: Israel." *Bureau of Public Affairs.* Retrieved May 16, 2014, from http://www.state.gov/r/pa/ei/bgn/3581.htm.

U.S. Department of State. (2014). "Background Note: Italy." *Bureau of Public Affairs.* Retrieved May 20, 2014, from http://www.state.gov/r/pa/ei/bgn/4033.htm.

U.S. Department of State. (2014). "Background Note: Jamaica." *Bureau of Public Affairs.* Retrieved May 12, 2014, from http://www.state.gov/r/pa/ei/bgn/2032.htm.

U.S. Department of State. (2014). "Background Note: Japan." *Bureau of Public Affairs.* Retrieved May 28, 2014, from http://www.state.gov/r/pa/ei/bgn/4142.htm.

U.S. Department of State. (2014). "Background Note: Kenya." *Bureau of Public Affairs.* Retrieved April 14, 2014, from http://www.state.gov/r/pa/ei/bgn/2962.htm.

U.S. Department of State. (2014). "Background Note: Morocco." *Bureau of Public Affairs*. Retrieved April 14, 2014, from http://www.state.gov/r/pa/ei/bgn/5431.htm.

U.S. Department of State. (2014). "Background Note: Nicaragua." *Bureau of Public Affairs*. Retrieved May 14, 2014, from http://www.state.gov/r/pa/ei/bgn/1850.htm.

U.S. Department of State. (2014). "Background Note: North Korea." *Bureau of Public Affairs*. Retrieved May 11, 2014, from http://www.state.gov/r/pa/ei/bgn/2792.htm.

U.S. Department of State. (2014). "Background Note: Senegal." *Bureau of Public Affairs*. Retrieved April 14, 2014, from http://www.state.gov/r/pa/ei/bgn/2862.htm.

U.S. Department of State. (2014). "Background Note: South Africa." *Bureau of Public Affairs*. Retrieved April 21, 2014, from http://www.state.gov/r/pa/ei/bgn/2898.htm.

U.S. Department of State. (2014). "Background Note: South Korea." *Bureau of Public Affairs*. Retrieved April 29, 2014, from http://www.state.gov/r/pa/ei/bgn/2800.htm.

U.S. Department of State. (2014). "Background Note: Trinidad and Tobago." *Bureau of Public Affairs*. Retrieved May 12, 2014, from http://www.state.gov/r/pa/ei/bgn/35638.htm.

U.S. Department of State. (2014). "Background Note: Turkey." *Bureau of Public Affairs*. Retrieved May 17, 2014, from http://www.state.gov/r/pa/ei/bgn/3432.htm.

Yenen, Serif. (2014). "Family. Turkish Odyssey." Retrieved May 17, 2014, from http://www.turkishodyssey.com/turkey/culture/people.htm#FAMILY.

ABOUT THE AUTHOR

Dr. Paula Saine is the co-chair of the Department of Teacher Education (EDT) at Miami University in Oxford, Ohio, and the president of the Ohio Council for the International Reading Association (OCIRA), and has over thirty years of teaching experience in K–16 settings and beyond. She served as coordinator of Digital Expo, a conference in which university faculty, students, and classroom teachers across southwest Ohio presented creative, scholarly, and pedagogical projects on technology. Her scholarly work is connected to three subjects: literacy, culture, and the use of technology in the classroom. These interests have resulted in numerous international presentations and professional workshops that span from Cuba and Jamaica to The Gambia, Nigeria, and Mauritius in Africa, to London, England. She has published widely on preparing quality teachers of literacy, e-mentoring in K–12, and using technology to enhance reading and writing in the classroom. Her current research centers on the extent to which a blended (face-to-face and online) tutoring model enhances literacy learning of fifth- and sixth-grade struggling readers and writers.

Dr. Saine is the associate editor of the *International Journal of Learning*. She has served as an editorial review board member for *The Teacher Educator, Balanced Reading Instruction, Negro Education Review*, and *Journal of Reading Education*. She also serves as the editor of the technology column for the *New England Journal of Reading Association* and is a program reviewer for the International Reading Association/National Council for Accreditation of Teacher Education (IRA/NCATE) as well as an IRA conference proposal reviewer. She currently serves as an Ambassador for International Affairs for the Greater Cincinnati chapter of the International Reading Association.